FAMILY MONEY MANAGEMENT GOD'S WAY

LIVE ABUNDANTLY, FREE FROM DEBT

BY MAHLON HETRICK OF Christian Financial Counseling

BARBOUR
PUBLISHING

Cover design by Priority Marketing, Fort Myers, Florida.

Published by Barbour Publishing, Inc., P.O. Box 719, Uhrichsville, Ohio 44683, www.barbourbooks.com

Our mission is to publish and distribute inspirational products offering exceptional value and biblical encouragement to the masses.

 Member of the Evangelical Christian Publishers Association

Printed in the United States of America.

ACKNOWLEDGMENTS

I would like to express my thanks and appreciation to many who have made this book possible.

To God for His wisdom, understanding, direction, love, mercy, forgiveness, experience, opportunities, and for His many blessings, especially during the past twenty-six years of this ministry.

To my loving wife, Marlyn, who for fifty-four years has been my wife, my best friend, my encourager, my inspiration, and my understanding companion.

To my three wonderful sons, Gary, Daniel, and Kenneth, who gave me the challenge, opportunity, and experience of being a father.

To Hugh Barbour, the founder of Barbour Publishing, for his challenge to me to write this book.

To my parents, who are now with the Lord, for their love, guidance, and influence in my life.

To the board members and staff of Christian Financial Counseling for the many hours of volunteer time they give to serve the Lord and specifically this ministry.

To the four financial institutions for my thirty years of banking experience.

To the thousands of people God has placed in my path who gave me the experiences related in this book.

To Debbie Rogers, the capable office manager of Christian Financial Counseling, for her untiring devoted contributions in serving the Lord and helping to prepare this book.

INTRODUCTION

This book was written to provide a complete do-it-yourself budget workbook based on godly principles. The contents are derived from my thirty years of banking experience plus twenty-six years of counseling and teaching the Bible as a book of finance.

At this time of economic uncertainty, more and more individuals, families, and businesses are seeking advice to help them make sound financial decisions. Demands for seminars, workshops, speaking engagements, and counseling are steadily increasing. More and more radio and television programs are talking about the problems and solutions to our so-called money problems.

I believe that every problem has a solution and that God has the answer to every problem. The purpose of this book is to help you to understand God's principles for managing money in a commonsense, practical way, and then to show you how to apply those principles in an everyday plan called a budget.

Listening to God and obeying Him should result in greater joy, peace, and contentment in regard to your finances. The godly principles in this book have already helped hundreds of people become debt free, and thousands more are now working on their plans.

This book was written for all people who want to please God and bring glory to Him in every area of their lives, including the way they manage the possessions God has entrusted to them. It is also written for those who are struggling with finances, considering bankruptcy, or facing possible foreclosure, repossession, or suit.

We love you in the Lord, and our prayer is that we can help you to experience God's best for you.

Mahlon L. Hetrick, Christian Financial Counseling, Inc.

RESULTS OF READING THIS BOOK

- One counselee reduced debts by $45,000 in sixty days.
- A single mom became debt free in just a few weeks.
- A divorced mother of three reduced monthly debt payments from $640 per month to $300 per month.
- One couple avoided bankruptcy and improved their finances in just one year.
- Another couple started tithing, started saving, and reduced debt payments by nearly $1,500 per month—and it happened in only three months.
- Another couple paid $50,000 of credit card debt in three years. They started tithing on gross rather than net income, started saving for retirement and their children's college education, paid cash for vacations, and are now debt free except for their mortgage.
- One person said, "I can't seem to put your financial advice book down. We never realized how much God refers to money management in His Word."
- Another commented, "We still thank and praise the Lord for causing us to turn to your ministry five years ago. What a blessed change in our financial lives. We can talk to each other about finances now. Thank you and God—again!"
- One pastor said that after his church members attended the CFC seminar, people straightened out their financial priorities and put an end to shady business deals. God then started blessing them in marvelous ways for their obedience.
- One pastor said their weekly receipts were 47 percent greater for the three months following the seminar compared with the three months before the seminar.
- Another church that had to cut all staff members' salaries by 10 percent before the seminar due to a lack of funds became debt free in just two years after the seminar. They then started three missionary churches over the next five years, paying cash for the buildings and paying the salaries of the three pastors.
- One church leader wrote, "Praise God for the most successful seminar conducted in our church. I have received only favorable comments from those who attended."

CONTENTS

LIST OF FORMS

LIST OF FIGURES

FINANCIAL BONDAGE

You know you are in financial bondage when:

- You are not putting God first with your tithe.
- You are borrowing to buy a want or a luxury.
- You are not able to pay all your bills on time.
- Your outgo exceeds your income.
- You do not have a balanced budget.
- You are receiving delinquent letters or phone calls.
- You are not saving for the future.
- You borrow from one lender to pay another lender.
- You are not being honest about your finances.
- You are using your reserves to pay for your overspending.
- Money problems are destroying your marriage.

A GREAT WAY TO PREVENT MONEY PROBLEMS

Adopt the following attitude:

Use it up! Wear it out!
Make it do! Or do without!

PART 1: FOUNDATIONS

CHAPTER 1
IDENTIFY THE PROBLEM

Approximately 80 percent of the people who seek financial counsel think they have a money problem because their outgo exceeds their income. They are looking for corrective counsel to solve their so-called money problem. Not one person has a money problem; we just think we do. **You cannot solve the problem until you identify it.** If your car will not start, you need to identify the problem and treat the cause of the problem before it is solved. The same is true with your finances.

What Kind of Problems Do We Have?

What is our problem if our outgo exceeds our income and we are living from payday to payday and not able to save for the future or pay our bills on time or enjoy the good things in life? Our problem falls into two general categories: ignorance and wrong attitudes.

Ignorance

We went to school and learned all the skills to earn a living, but most of us were not required to take even one course on how to manage money after we have earned it. We are not dumb, but we are ignorant. Based on your income, how much can you afford to spend for housing, food, transportation, insurance, entertainment, and so on? Many people don't know the answer to that question and don't even know where to go to get guidelines. You can graduate with a Ph.D. in finance and not know how to put together, organize, analyze, and control a family budget.

Most people who think they have a budget are just record keepers. Some people are good record keepers, some are poor record keepers, and some don't even keep any records at all. A budget is a written plan to determine how income will be allocated in a proper balance to meet all one's needs and goals.

Wrong Attitudes

We are made up of two things: our attitudes and our actions. Great philosophers have said, "We become what we think." God says in Proverbs 23:7 (KJV), *"For as he thinketh in his heart, so is he."* We do what we think; our actions are a result of our thinking. We don't have a money problem—we have an attitude problem regarding money and money matters.

Our attitude problem may involve some of the following:

Pride. "I am too proud to live in an old house, drive an old car, or wear old clothes. I want the nicest, newest, biggest, and best, whether I can afford them or not. After all, I don't want anybody to think I'm not successful." God says we are to be humble, not proud.

Greed. "I am going to get what I want. The world's attitude is 'whoever gets the most toys wins,' so I am going to gather my toys whether I can afford them or not." God says we are to be generous, not greedy.

Covetousness. "I want what other people have. I want to keep up with the neighbors, my peers, my family. I want to keep up with 'the Joneses.'" You don't have to worry about keeping up with the Joneses. I saw it on a very reliable source—an old episode of *The Flintstones.* Fred said the Joneses had just declared bankruptcy, so we don't need to worry about keeping up with the Joneses any longer. God says we should not covet what our neighbors have.

Lack of Discipline. Discipline is simply setting the rules and then following them. If we do not set rules and follow rules to live within our income, we are living within our credit. The average family in the United States is spending 122 percent of its income. Business failures have doubled in the past ten years, due to businesses spending more money than they make. We are the government, and since 1934, we have been spending more money than we receive in revenues. Individuals, families, businesses, and government are all going one way—the wrong way. God told us in Proverbs 21:20 (TLB), *"The wise man saves for the future, but the foolish man spends whatever he gets."* We are not wise (spending less than we get); we are not even foolish (spending everything we get); we are *more than foolish* (spending beyond our income). If we want to be wise, our attitude should be to fix our spending level below our income level and save from our abundance for the future.

Discipline is a very positive word because it is necessary to reach our goals. Without discipline no athlete is a winner—that is, reaches his or her goal. Without discipline (rules and following the rules), we have no peace in the world. Without discipline (rules and following the rules), we have no education in the classroom. Without discipline (rules and following the rules), we have no safety on the highways. Why do we think we can earn and spend money with no rules, guidelines, or budget and still reach our goals? We can't. We must have the discipline of a written plan, a budget. Lack of discipline is a serious attitude problem. God says we are to save for the future, and the only way we can do that is to discipline ourselves to spend less than we receive. A budget helps us to do that.

Lack of Contentment. We are the most discontent, dissatisfied nation in the world. We want bigger, better, and more of the latest fashions, models, and styles. How do we know we are discontent? Did the family who bought their last house buy it because their old house was falling down or no longer livable? Did the person who bought his latest car buy it because his old car would not go one more mile and could not be repaired? Did the person who bought clothes recently buy them because all she had in the closet were rags and hangers?

It is very doubtful that is the reason they made their purchases. You see, we are not content, so we buy bigger, better, and more. Paul said in the New Testament that *whether he had much or little, he was content* (Phil. 4:11). God is telling us to be content with what He provides.

You Think You Owe It to Yourself. The new-car salesperson tells you, "You look great in that luxury coupe. You owe it to yourself. Go ahead and buy it." The salesperson in the exclusive dress shop tells you, "You look elegant in that $350 dress. You owe it to yourself. Go ahead and buy it."

If you buy everything from people who tell you, "You owe it to yourself," you will find out whom you really owe it to—Visa, MasterCard, this bank, or that merchant. Proverbs 21:2 (TLB) tells us, *"We can justify our every deed but God looks at our motives."* Are we simply trying to justify buying luxurious, extravagant items? God says we are to be diligent and wise managers, and to do what is right for the right reasons.

What Causes the Problems?

We are ignorant because we have not been taught. Our schools are not teaching students how to manage money after they earn it. Our churches are not teaching people how to manage money in the home. **The Bible is the best book on finance ever written. God has more to say in the Bible about money than any other subject except love.** But are we looking in the Bible for direction? Are we listening to God? If we don't know the Bible is the best book on finances ever written, we won't go to it for information or direction in money matters.

We have wrong attitudes because of what we have experienced. The world's way encourages us to be proud, greedy, covetous, and discontent, and to spend without discipline. We experience borrow-borrow, spend-spend, operate on other people's money, gain leverage, get easy credit, pay it back with cheaper dollars. When we listen to the world's ways and ignore God's ways, we have wrong attitudes that cause a money problem.

Summary

1. We must identify the problem to solve it.
2. We have ignorance problems and attitude problems that result in money problems.
3. God's ways are not the world's ways, and we are at a fork in the road. We need to make a decision; we can't avoid making a decision. Will it be the right decision? God's way or the world's way?

"Real-Life Results from CFC Counselees"

ATTITUDE

A couple said as soon as they changed their attitude about money and realized that God was the owner of everything, they began to see God work in their lives. In the past they had overspent, over invested, and lived from paycheck to paycheck. They had credit card debt, medical bills, personal loans, and car loans. After counseling they sold their house, moved into a small condo. . .and tore up their credit cards. . .paid off personal debts and car loans. . .and set up a budget based on the husband's income alone. Then they both felt an overwhelming peace and freedom in their lives.

CHAPTER 2
FIND SOLUTIONS

Set Financial Goals

We can't get to where we are going until we know where we want to go. Setting goals is the first step toward reaching them. Most of us will have many goals—some immediate and short-range, others long-range for the future. **Every Christian should set goals that bring glory to God and that meet personal and family needs.** Every step in financial planning should be written, starting with a budget.

Where do we start? Make a list of short-range goals that you want to accomplish this month or this year: for example, pay all bills on time, start a savings account, increase giving to God, and so on. Next, make a list of long-range goals: for example, save to replace a car in three years and pay cash for it; save for a down payment on a home; save for children's college education; provide adequate life insurance and health insurance; save for retirement; execute a will that honors God and provides for the family. Both short- and long-range goals will grow as you continue to revise the list. Proverbs 29:18 (KJV) says, *"Where there is no vision [goals], the people perish."*

Establish Priorities

Many times we have more dreams and goals than we can reach at one time. In our monthly budgets, we may run short of funds to accomplish everything in one month. When this happens, we need to look over our written list and establish priorities. A simple procedure could be to check off all the items that are absolute needs. Then as funds permit, add wants. **Keep in mind that our first priority is to honor God.** Then we are to meet our obligations to the government. And the balance—which we call "net spendable"—is the discretionary amount for us to allocate to the remainder of our budget items.

Develop a Written Plan (Budget)

A budget is a written plan to determine how income will be allocated in a proper balance so that all the needs of the family will be met after honoring God and paying your taxes. This plan should result in peace, contentment, and joy over money matters, not worry, fear, frustration, and family arguments. Many sources report that more than 50 percent of all marriages end up in divorce court in five years, and the major reason for divorce is money and money-related matters. **Only God knows how many marriages could be saved if families would only establish and follow a budget based on God's guidelines.** I sometimes believe that young married couples are deaf. They thought the minister said, "Until *debt* do us part." Proverbs 16:9 (TLB) says, *"We should make plans—counting on God to direct us."*

Take Action (Start Now!)

We can know where we want to go, but we are not going to get there until we take action. The first step is to make plans to reach our goals. Our budget is our written plan. Remember, if it doesn't work on paper, it will not work in reality. The second step is to activate the plan by recording all income and outgo, day by day and category by category. The forms provided in this budget workbook will help you organize and activate a budget. We strongly encourage you to use them and follow their instructions. **Procrastination is the number one reason for financial failure**. One definition of *success* is "Do it now." We are to be *"doers of the word, and not hearers only"* (James 1:22 KJV). So let us get started doing those things that will lead us to being successful money managers for God.

Commit to Follow the Plan

A commitment is a decision. We are at another fork in the road. When we have a choice of two options, we can't avoid making a decision. **We must decide whether to follow the plan** or not to follow the plan. If we don't follow the plan, we have wasted our time developing it. If we don't follow the plan, our goals, visions, and dreams will never become real. God wants us to give our best and succeed, not give our second best and fail. One of the biggest problems in our society today is broken promises. We promise or commit to doing something, but then we don't do it. Proverbs 16:3 (TLB) says, *"Commit your work to the Lord, then it will succeed."* And in Ecclesiastes 5:5 (TLB) we are cautioned, *"It is far better not to say you'll do something than to say you will and then not do it."*

Modify the Plan

If and when circumstances change, we may need to modify our budget plan. When we receive a raise, we need to allocate where we are going to apply the additional funds in our budget. If we have an unplanned expense or we experience a reduced income, we need to reassess our expenditures. We may receive an inheritance, a large gift, or a big bonus; these are other reasons to modify our plan. **Our overall goal should be to get out of debt and stay out of debt**. Each modification should support that goal. Another goal should be to save for the future, so our modified plan should always include spending less than we have coming in so that we can have an abundance from which we can save for the future. The apostle Paul admonishes in Romans 13:8 (KJV), *"Owe no man any thing."* And Proverbs 21:20 (TLB) teaches, *"The wise man saves for the future, but the foolish man spends whatever he gets."*

Summary

We need to have written goals, both short- and long-range. We must establish priorities and allocate to each goal based on our needs first, then our wants. Then we develop a budget, which is a written plan to determine how much money is allocated to each category and each item within that category. **Remember, our goal throughout the entire procedure is to bring glory to God** as we plan to be wise and faithful stewards.

Next we need to put our plans into action and, most important, follow them, so that we can reach our goals and be the successes that God wants us to be and that we want to be. Then, if and when circumstances change, we need to be flexible and modify our plans to stay on course so we still reach our goals—sometimes sooner, sometimes later.

"REAL-LIFE RESULTS FROM CFC COUNSELEES"

CUT EXPENSES

In looking back, I see what a wonderful thing God has done for us. In one year, we reduced our debt by one-half and we received several unexpected bonuses. I revamped the way I grocery shopped and have cut that expense in half and because I purchased fewer prepackaged foods, I have lost 25 pounds. This December was our first ever cash only Christmas—it was the best holiday and there was no dread of bills coming in January!

CHAPTER 3
HOW TO FIND AN ABUNDANCE
IN YOUR BUDGET

Tragically, most people do not know how to find an abundance in their budgets, and they are going to the wrong source. They are not listening to what God has to say. If they turned to Matthew 25:29 (TLB), they would find that it says, *"For the man who uses well what he is given shall be given more, and he shall have abundance."* What Jesus is saying is that the man who manages well is the one who is going to have an abundance. Too often we listen to what the world says when we ought to be listening to God. Jesus does not say in this verse that the person who is born in the right home, has the right job, goes to the right school, lives in the right country, or is in the right place at the right time is the one who is going to have an abundance. He says, *"For the man who uses well. . .shall have abundance."*

As I said earlier, although we are taught skills to earn a living, most of us have not been taught how to manage money after we have earned it. We need to know the answers to questions such as these: What percentage of my budget can be spent for clothing? For food? For transportation? For entertainment? For housing? How much can I afford to spend in these various areas and have a balanced budget and be a good manager? Many of us don't even know where to get the answers to these questions. A person can graduate with a Ph.D. in finance and still not know how to put together a family budget, analyze a budget, or set up a system of budget control. We send people into outer space, we have built a global audio and video communication system, yet we have failed to teach our families—God's first institution and the backbone of our nation—how to be good managers, which God says is the key to having an abundance.

We all seem to struggle along and learn from trial and error or from other people. Some of us even learn Thomas Edison's way—finding 999 ways how *not* to do something before we finally learn how to do it. It is tragic that we make so many mistakes. I have counseled with people that have gone through loan consolidations two, three, or four times; some have been in financial trouble for twenty years and still have not learned how to do it. They keep doing the same thing over and over because they are treating symptoms, not solving problems.

Consider the parable of the talents in Matthew 25:14–30. To the first the master gave five talents, and the servant doubled it; to the second the master gave two talents, and the servant doubled it; to the third the master gave one talent, and the servant buried it. When the master returned, he said to the servant who turned five talents into ten, "Well done, good and faithful servant. Since you managed well, I will entrust to you more, and it will be a joyous task" (my paraphrase). He said the same thing to the servant who had two talents and ended up with four. The master was not concerned with how much the servants had in the beginning, but with how well they managed whatever they had. And to the one who had one talent and buried it, he said, "Wicked man, lazy slave, at least you should have put the money in the bank and earned interest. Since you haven't done that, I'm going to take it from you and give it to the one who has the ten and knows how to manage" (my paraphrase), and that is what he did.

What is Jesus teaching in this parable? In the beginning, He says the master gave different amounts according to the servants' abilities. Abilities to do what? To manage! God is not going to give everybody the same amount, so we should not be envious of people who have more; nor should we look down on those who have less. It does not necessarily mean that one is in sin because he has less and the other is being blessed of God because he has more. That is not the case. If the amount of money and possessions we have are in direct relationship to our spiritual growth and obedience, then why were the disciples so poor, and why did Jesus have nothing but the clothing on His back? Let us be careful that we do not misunderstand. Yes, God does expect us to be good managers, but having material wealth is not an indication that we are spiritual or godly. We may be godly, but material wealth is not necessarily the only measure of this.

Jesus is also teaching that the way we manage determines whether we have joy. If we manage well, we will have more, and it will be a joy. If we blow it and mismanage, we will lose what we have. God expects us to use wisely what He has entrusted to us; He expects us to invest it. He expects us to put it to work and make it grow, not bury it.

The bottom line of this parable is found in Matthew 25:29, and we ought to plant it firmly in our minds. **The person who manages well what he or she is given is going to be given more and will have an abundance.** Keep in mind that God's wealth is not limited to material things. God's idea of prosperity includes material things but is not limited to them. **God's wealth also includes our salvation, our health, our family, our friends, our love, joy, peace, contentment, and other things that we cannot buy with money.**

God Is the Owner

For more than thirty years as a Christian, I did not understand that God owned everything. I thought I owned the house I lived in because my name was on the deed. I paid for it with the money I earned. The same with my car: My name was on the title; I paid for it with the money I earned. These were my clothes. I bought them with my money. I, I, I, I!

When I read and understood God's Word, I discovered that I was wrong. For example, in Psalm 50:10–12 (TLB) I read, *"For all the animals of field and forest are mine! The cattle on a thousand hills! . . . All the world is mine, and everything in it."* God did not say, "everything except." In 1 Chronicles 29:11, 14 (TLB), King David proclaims, *"Everything in the heavens and earth is yours, O Lord, and this is your kingdom. . . . Everything we have has come from you, and we only give you what is yours already!"* There is not a thing we can give God that is not already His. And then, for those who think their money does not belong to God, I found in Haggai 2:8 (KJV), *"The silver is mine, and the gold is mine, saith the Lord of hosts."* My favorite is 1 Corinthians 10:26 (TLB), which says, *"For the earth and every good thing in it belongs to the Lord and is yours to enjoy."*

God is the owner of everything, and He has entrusted an amount to us while we are passing through this life so that we can enjoy it. If you and I are not enjoying what God has entrusted to us, guess what? It is not His fault. That is when we need to look in the mirror and be honest with ourselves and say, "God, what are You telling me? Do You want me to change my attitude, my lifestyle, my priorities, my value system? What do You want me to change so that I can enjoy what You have entrusted to me?" Approximately 80 percent of the people who come for counseling have reached a point of frustration because their outgo exceeds their income. They are not enjoying what God has entrusted to them. One of the greatest needs today is to share with people from God's Word how to manage money so they can understand God's plan, receive God's best, and enjoy what He owns and has entrusted to them.

We read in 1 Timothy 6:7 (KJV), *"For we brought nothing into this world, and it is certain we can carry nothing out."* In the same vein, Billy Graham has said, "You never saw a hearse going to a cemetery pulling a U-Haul." We are not going to take anything with us. God is telling us that money has no spiritual value. If it did, He would have enabled us to take it with us to heaven.

So, what is money? Money is simply a tool for us to manage while we are passing through this life. A hammer is a tool. You can use a hammer to build or destroy. Likewise, money is a tool. You can use it for good or evil—to build or destroy. The attitude of the person in control of the tools determines how the tools are going to be used. We are in control of what God has entrusted to us, and it is up to us to do things either God's way or the world's way. The decision is ours.

Where are we going for counseling? Where are we going for instructions and training, for money-management guidelines and principles? Most everyone has already been to the world dozens of times, trying to find the answers. Since God has more to say in the Bible about money than any other subject except love, we need to listen to what He is communicating to us. But do we care enough about what God is saying to open our Bibles?

We Are the Managers

If God is the owner and we are the managers, or stewards, we need to know what a steward does. A simple definition of a steward is "one who manages that which belongs to another." In our case, **God is the owner, and we are managing what belongs to Him**. In 1 Corinthians 4:2 (KJV), Paul tells us what kind of character stewards must have: *"Moreover it is required in stewards [managers], that a man be found faithful."* A synonym for "faithful" is true. To what are we to be faithful and true? To God's Word, God's way, and God's will for our lives. But we can't be faithful and true to God's Word and ways as they relate to managing money if we have not been taught and do not understand what God is saying. Thus, we need to know what God's Word has to say about managing money.

God rewards our faithfulness, not our perfection. So if you are not perfect in your budget, if you are not perfect in what you are doing, don't get upset. God looks at the heart. He knows what you are trying to do, that you are trying your best to be faithful, trying to listen to what He has to say, and trying to be obedient. He wants us to give our best to Him, to excel as we manage for Him.

Our Purpose—To Glorify God

What is our purpose? God's will for your life is different than His will for my life. But God's purpose for every Christian is the same. God's *purpose* for you and me is to bring glory to God, to please Him, to honor Him, and to obey Him. First Peter 4:11 (KJV) says, *"If any man minister. . ."* A minister is a servant. Christ came to serve, not to be served. If we are Christians, we are to be Christlike—or like Christ. We are here to serve. And if we are here to serve, we are to give our best. As we continue to read this verse, it tells us how to do it. *"Do it as of the ability which God giveth."* Why do you think God wants us to serve and excel by doing God's given ability? So everyone can pat us on the back and tell us how great we are? No, that is not why. We need to finish the verse. We are to do it *"that God in all things may be glorified."* As Christians, our purpose is to glorify God every day in every way by obeying Him and His ways, including the way we manage our money. Let's be sure we are reading the Bible to find out God's ways to manage money.

Many of us have problems, including problems in finance. God says in Psalm 50:15 (TLB), *"I want you to trust me in your times of trouble, [Why?] so I can rescue you, [Why?] and you can give me glory."* When we have a problem, God doesn't want us to trust ourselves. He wants us to turn to Him, to communicate with Him by praying and seeking answers through reading His Word and through teaching, preaching, counseling, and being helped by others. If you need to talk with God, just give Him a call. He has a phone number—Jeremiah 33:3 (KJV), *"Call unto me, and I will answer thee, and shew thee great and mighty things, which thou knowest not."* God is saying that when you don't have the answers, when you don't know what to do, give Him a call.

And what is God going to tell you to do? He says in Proverbs 15:22 (NASB), *"Without consultation, plans are frustrated, but with many counselors they succeed."* If you want success, seek the counsel of many counselors. But be cautious about it. In Psalm 1:1 (KJV), we learn, *"Blessed is the man who walketh not in the counsel of the ungodly."* Do not go to ungodly people for counsel to learn how to bring glory to God, because ungodly people do not understand that God is the owner and that we are simply the managers and our purpose is to bring glory to Him. They can't help us bring glory to God in our finances if they don't understand what bringing glory to God is all about.

Some Christian businesspeople are not applying biblical principles in their businesses; they are not godly people. Godly people listen to and obey God. They apply God's principles in their lives daily. God does not bless our disobedience; it is our obedience that He blesses. We need to be very, very selective about where we get advice, and remember that **our best counselor is the almighty Counselor.** Your best counselor here on earth, for those of you who are married, is your spouse. They have lived with you the longest, they know you best, they usually understand the problem, and they should have the same goals. Nevertheless, when many families talk about money, conflict arises. It should not be that way. **If we are to bring glory to God in our money management, we ought to have harmony with our spouses. Husbands and wives should have a oneness of purpose and a oneness of spirit, working together as one**.

To bring glory to God, we need to have the right attitude, the right actions, and the right reactions. *"For as he thinketh in his heart, so is he"* (Proverbs 23:7 KJV). If our attitude and heart are right, then our actions will reflect our attitude. What determines our attitude? What determines whether we are going to hate or love, be honest or dishonest? Our experience. I can't change your attitude, but God can change it in a second. If we want an attitude change so that our actions are proper, then we need to check with God. We need to ask God what He would have us do as a manager of what belongs to Him. When God shares that information with us in His Word, the Bible, we are checking with the right counselor. He says in Proverbs 2:1 (TLB), *"Every young man who listens to me and obeys my instructions will be given wisdom and good sense."* **When you read the Bible, ask two questions: (1) God, what are You telling me? (What is the message?) and (2) What do You want me to do about it?** "I am listening, God; what is the message? You want me to obey Your instruction?" We need to be sure that what we are doing will bring glory to God and will please Him. **To have a proper attitude, we need to experience the relationship with God that we ought to have; and then the decisions and actions that follow will also be what God wants us to have.**

Some people today want to escape, hide, give up, become bitter, or blame everybody else. God says in Psalm 50:15

(TLB), *"I want you to trust me in your times of trouble, so I can rescue you."* Are we, in our times of trouble, letting our adversity be turned into a blessing by turning to God and trusting Him and seeking His direction? When we have adversity in our finances or adversity in our lives, we should ask the same two questions that we ask whenever we are reading God's Word: (1) God, what are You telling me? and (2) What do You want me to do about it? Through adversity God brought me into a ministry to help others. Through adversity this budget workbook was put together. Are we blaming God, or are we praising God for adversity? James 1:2 (RSV) says, *"Count it all joy, my brethren, when you meet various trials."* We don't always understand all the things that happen. In Proverbs 20:24 (TLB), God says, *"Since the Lord is directing our steps, why try to understand everything that happens along the way?"* I didn't understand why God called me into a ministry. I didn't understand why I had to get fired after thirty years in banking. I didn't understand why I had to go unemployed for eleven months. I didn't understand at the time. But now when I look back, I realize that it was the only way that God could get my attention and redirect my life. Maybe God is permitting adversity in your life to redirect your life. Just get excited about what He has in store for you. Don't look at it as adversity, but as a blessing in disguise. Getting fired was one of the greatest blessings in my life. I wouldn't be in this ministry today had I not been fired. I wasn't fired because I committed a crime. I was fired because it was God's plan.

In summary, we need to have the understanding and attitude that God is the owner of all things, that you and I are managers, and that our purpose as managers is to bring glory to God. That is the foundation on which to build and make any other decision in the area of finance, including budgeting.

Start by Earning an Honest Living

"God, where do we start?"

God tells us to start by earning an honest living. In Ephesians 4:28 (TLB), Paul admonishes, *"If anyone is stealing he must stop it and begin using those hands of his for honest work."* And Proverbs 13:11 (TLB) teaches, *"Wealth from gambling quickly disappears; wealth from hard work grows."* Honest, hard work is what God wants. He tells us in Proverbs 12:11 (TLB), *"Hard work means prosperity; only a fool idles away his time."* And in Proverbs 16:8 (TLB), He says, *"A little, gained honestly, is better than great wealth gotten by dishonest means."* The important thing is not how much we have, but whether we earned it God's way. Did we earn it honestly? *"It is a wonderful heritage to have an honest father"* (Proverbs 20:7 TLB). A greater heritage to leave to our children than wealth by the world's material standards is to leave them the reputation of honesty and the teaching and the training of what is right in the sight of God. Proverbs 21:2 (TLB) says, *"We can justify our every deed but God looks at our motives."* God looks not at what we do, our deeds, but at why we do what we do, our motives. **A lot of people are doing the right things, but often they are doing them for the wrong reasons.** They are not all managing it to bring glory to God or to honor Him. Some are doing it for greed and pride or for selfish pleasure. Another verse to go with Proverbs 21:2 is Proverbs 16:2 (TLB), which says, *"We can always 'prove' that we are right, but is the Lord convinced?"*

Honor the Lord

"After we earn money honestly, what do you want us to do, God?"

God tells us that He wants us to honor Him. How do we do that? Proverbs 3:9 (TLB) instructs, *"Honor the Lord by giving him the first part of all your income."* The King James translation of this verse says, *"Honour the LORD with thy substance [what we already have], and with the firstfruits of all thine increase."* God is telling us that we have two ways to honor Him. We can give to Him from what we already have, from our reserves, and we can give to Him from our increase. God also established the plan of regular systematic giving on the first day of the week. Now, God's Word does not say to honor the Lord by giving Him the first part of all your income *after taxes*. It does not say to honor the Lord by giving Him the first part of your income *unless you are in debt*, or *only if you are earning above poverty-level wages*, or *only as long as it is still tax deductible*. None of those conditions are part of God's plan. He says, "I want you to honor me regardless of the economic conditions of the land. And regardless of your personal situation, I want you to put Me first and honor Me." In Ephesians 6:2 (KJV), Paul tells us, *"Honour thy father and mother."* Children honor their parents by showing love to them through their obedience. Likewise, we honor God by showing our love for Him through our obedience. What are we to obey?

Proverbs 3:9 (TLB) says, *"Honor the Lord by giving him the first part of all your income."* Many people don't understand this. **We should give because we desire to honor the Lord. We have the freedom of choice to be obedient or to be disobedient.** Proverbs 13:13 (TLB) says, *"Despise God's Word and find yourself in trouble. Obey it and succeed."*

The consequences are that we will find ourselves in trouble if we continually choose to be disobedient to God, and we will have success if we choose to obey. God says that He wants us to bring the first part into the storehouse. He tells us in Malachi 3:10 (KJV), *"Bring ye all the tithes into the storehouse [the tithe is a tenth; the storehouse is the church]. . .and prove me now."* This is the only place in the Bible where God says, "Prove Me, try Me, test Me; see if I won't do what I tell you I will do." What does He say He will do? *"[See] if I will not open you the windows of heaven, and pour you out a blessing, that there shall not be room enough to receive it."* I believe God is saying," I love you; you are My child; I want to bless you. The prerequisite is obedience, bringing that first part into the storehouse." He is saying that when we do that, He will know that we recognize that He is the owner and we are the managers, and that we choose to be obedient managers by returning the first part to Him. I believe God designed this plan to give us an opportunity for Him to bless the 90 percent or less that we keep. Again, we display a loving attitude when we honor the Lord by choosing to obey Him and follow His Word. As 2 Corinthians 9:7 (KJV) says, ***"Every man according as he purposeth in his heart, so let him give; not grudgingly or of necessity: for God loveth a cheerful giver."***

"REAL-LIFE RESULTS FROM CFC COUNSELEES"
AFTER HONORING GOD
We believe in what you are doing at CFC. Before counseling we were giving $10/month, after counseling we committed to tithing and shortly thereafter, my husband received a 10% raise.

Pay Your Taxes

Now God says there is something else for us to do. Not only does He want us to earn money honestly and honor Him with the first part, but He wants us to support the government by paying our taxes. In Matthew 22:21 (KJV), Jesus says, *"Render therefore unto Caesar the things which are Caesar's; and unto God the things that are God's."* Jesus is saying that the act of giving to God and giving to the government is not an either/or matter; it is a matter of managing well so that we can do both. Proverbs 16:11 (TLB) says, *"The Lord demands fairness in every business deal. He established this principle."* God wants you to be fair to Him, to the government, and to your family. He wants you to be fair to your employer, your employees, and your creditors. If I have ten creditors and am paying only eight of them, I am being unfair to the other two. If I am being unfair to the other two, I am being disobedient to God's principle of fairness. Do I expect God's blessing when I am being disobedient? No. **Obedience is the key to prosperity.** God is telling us to be fair in every relationship. To be fair to family, we need to manage well in our home, and that is why a budget is needed.

Save for the Future

Proverbs 21:20 (TLB) points out that *"the wise man saves for the future, but the foolish man spends whatever he gets."* God's message to us here is that He wants us to fix our level of spending below our level of income. Why? So we can acquire a surplus. **The only way we can save for the future is from a surplus. God says we are foolish if we spend every penny we get.** As I noted earlier, the average family in the United States is spending 122 percent of its income, going deeper and deeper in debt, trying to live within its credit, not within its income. Businesses and government are doing the same thing. It appears that government, businesses, and families are going the wrong way on a one-way street.

This budget workbook should help you understand God's principle of living within your income. **We need to fix our spending level in our budget plan below our level of income so that we can be obedient to God and save for the future.** God also told us in Proverbs 6:6 (TLB), *"Take a lesson from the ants, you lazy fellow. Learn from their ways and be wise!"* What do ants do? When there is a surplus of food in the summertime, they store up for the uncertain future. And guess what? There is no king ant or queen ant giving instructions. Without being told, the ant is saving for the uncertain future. We should do the same.

"REAL-LIFE RESULTS FROM CFC COUNSELEES"
AFTER SAVING FOR THE FUTURE
Another couple was barely surviving from one paycheck to another. After attending a CFC seminar and making a decision to manage money God's way they are now debt free and are saving for the future. Best of all they accepted Jesus as their Lord and Savior!

Provide for Your Family

There are a lot of good reasons to save, one of which can be found in 1 Timothy 5:8 (TLB): *"Anyone who won't care for his own relatives [When?] when they need help, especially those living in his own family, has no right to say he is a Christian. Such a person is worse than the heathen."* Jesus says in John 15:12 (TLB), *"I demand that you love each other as much as I love you."* Loving is not an option. He also tells us in John 13:34 (TLB), *"I am giving a new commandment to you now—love each other just as much as I love you."* He adds in the next verse, *"Your strong love for each other will prove to the world that you are my disciples"* (v. 35 TLB). And three times **Jesus says that the demonstration of our love for Him is our obedience**: *"If you love me, obey me"* (John 14:15 TLB); *"The one who obeys me is the one who loves me"* (v. 21 TLB); and *"Anyone who doesn't obey me doesn't love me."* (v. 24 TLB).

God is saying, "Just do what I am asking you to do." What is God asking us to do? Well, He is asking us to understand, first of all, that He is the owner and that we are the managers. Our purpose is to bring glory to Him, to earn money honestly, to return to the Lord the first part of what we earn, to give the government its share, and to save some for the future so that we can provide for family and help others in need. Jesus said, *"It is more blessed to give than to receive"* (Acts 20:35 KJV). God wants to bless us, but when we mismanage and do not have anything to give, we rob ourselves of the blessing God intended us to have. If we don't obey God and provide for family, we don't love Him. If we don't love our family, God's love is not in our hearts. So, we have a responsibility to provide for family. No place in the Bible does it say that when we have a need we should go to the government or to the bank. It tells us that family should help family. That is God's way.

Give to the Needy

Paul exhorts us in Ephesians 4:28 (KJV), *"Let him that stole steal no more: but rather let him labour, working with his hands the thing which is good, [Why?] that he may have [Why?] to give to him that needeth."* We are to give not to the greedy, but to the needy—those who can't help themselves.

If we are in a situation where we have a so-called financial problem, God is expecting us to do everything we can to manage well first. We are not needy until we have done everything we can do.

A lot of people are poor because they are lazy. Others are poor because they are poor managers. Still others are poor because they don't want to seek counsel. All they want is for somebody to give them a fish every day. They don't want someone to teach them to fish, because then they would have to go to work. We need to be sure in our budget planning that we do everything we can do God's way to help ourselves first. When we have done all we can, we need to trust God. In Psalm 50:15 (TLB), God says, *"I want you to trust me in your times of trouble, [Why?] so I can rescue you."* We see God rescuing people all the time in our financial counseling ministry, with unexpected loans, gifts coming from unexpected places, and debts forgiven. Many wonderful things are happening to our counselees, including avoiding bankruptcies, foreclosures, repossessions, and suits, and even stopping divorces and suicides. God does not deal the same way with everyone. He may want us to go through struggling for a longer period of time in our problem area. It took me eleven months in my valley until God called me into the ministry and gave me the direction He wanted me to take. In my thirty years of banking, I was never debt free, but in my eleven months of unemployment, I became totally debt free. Why? I stopped trusting the world and the world's way of borrowing money, and I started trusting God. God released money that was restricted, money that was not to be available for two more years. He released it and permitted me to become debt free and remain debt free since 1982. I am now trusting God so I will never have to borrow any money the rest of my life. I am not independently wealthy; I'm just trusting God. God wants us to save so we can help each other.

Seven Steps for Good Management

I encourage you to read and reread the following seven steps for good money management.

Step 1: Make Plans

In Proverbs 16:9 (TLB), we read, *"We should make plans—counting on God to direct us."* A budget is a written plan to determine how the money that comes into the home is going to be allocated in a proper balance to honor the Lord, meet all our needs, and reach our goals. Everything should be in a proper balance with no frustration, worry, or fears about money. God is saying that we ought to have a budget, "counting on God to direct us." How can we count on God to direct us?

Step 2: Trust God

God tells us in Proverbs 3:5–6 (KJV), *"Trust in the LORD with all thine heart; and lean not unto thine own understanding. In all thy ways acknowledge him, [And what will happen?] and he shall direct thy paths."* God said that if we meet the two prerequisites—place our trust in Him (not in ourselves, not in our understanding, but in His understanding) and acknowledge Him in all our ways (put God first in every area of our life, including finances), then He will direct our paths. **God is telling us to be orderly, gather facts, seek counsel.**

Step 3: Be Orderly

God says that He want us to do all things in an orderly fashion. First Corinthians 14:40 (NASB) says, *"All things must be done properly and in an orderly manner."* That is what a budget helps us do.

Step 4: Gather Facts

Then God tells us to gather the facts: *"What a shame—yes, how stupid!—to decide before knowing the facts!"* (Proverbs 18:13 TLB). God is warning us not to make a decision before we gather all the information we need to make a wise decision.

Step 5: Seek Counsel

If we still don't know what to do, we are to seek counsel. *"Without consultation, plans are frustrated, but with many counselors they succeed"* (Proverbs 15:22 NASB). In Psalm 1:1 (KJV), God cautions: *"Blessed is the man that walketh not in the counsel of the ungodly."* We are to seek counsel from the godly, those who follow God's ways and God's Word, if we want to be blessed.

Step 6: Commit

Proverbs 16:3 (TLB) gives us this direction: *"Commit your work to the Lord, then it will succeed."* We could know all of the verses in the Bible, study them, memorize them, teach them, and even be hired as a consultant, but we still will not have solved one problem until we have committed our work to the Lord. Commit your work to the Lord today. Make a list of everything you possess, and then sign a statement saying, **"I now transfer the ownership of everything back to God."** Then pray the following:

> *Forgive me, Lord, for thinking I was the owner and acting like the owner. Now that I understand that You are the owner and I am the manager, just help me to manage in a way that brings glory to You, help me to earn it honestly, honor You with the first part, give to the government, provide for my family, save for the future, help others in need, and then, Lord, help me to follow Your steps of being a good manager.*

It is at this point that I have seen lives changed and marriages on the rocks being brought back together. One year after counseling, one young couple said, "We didn't know marriage could be so beautiful. Since we have our finances straightened out, we are enjoying marriage." God has a lot of fringe benefits in store for us—love, joy, peace, and contentment—none of which we can buy. If we will only listen to Him and be obedient, He has blessings and prosperity in store. We encourage you to pray for God's wisdom and understanding so that you can make right decisions. God already knows whether we are going to make it, if we have made it, or when we are going to make it. We don't ask for a show of hands or signed statements. It is between you and God.

Some people realize at this point that they have not received the gift of salvation by accepting Christ as their Savior. That is the most important decision a person can make, and it establishes a personal relationship with God. If you have any questions or would like to know how to be assured of eternal life with God, we would be pleased to help you (please see our contact information at the back of this book), or you can seek help from another Christian or minister.

What if a person decides to start managing money God's way and has a whole stack of bills he or she can't pay? What is that person to do? God tells us in Psalm 50:15, *"I want you to trust me in your times of trouble, so I can rescue you"* (TLB). Then in Proverbs 13:13, we see we have a choice: *"Despise God's word and find yourself in trouble. Obey it and succeed"* (TLB). To be successful we need to trust and obey God's word. Since many people worry over money troubles, God tells us in Matthew 6:34, *"Don't be anxious (worried) about tomorrow. God will take care of your tomorrow too. Live one day at a time"* (TLB). Simply put your worries in God's "worry basket." It appears that He is telling us to take one day at a time, trusting and obeying Him. Stop worrying and leave the blessings up to Him. What will happen when we do that?

Step 7: Obey God

God gives us a promise. He tells us in Proverbs 16:20, *"God blesses those who obey Him; happy is the man who puts his trust in the Lord"* (TLB). **God is saying that blessings and joy will be ours when we obey Him and put our trust in Him. And God keeps His promises!**

We are in the OBEDIENCE department
and God is in the BLESSING department.
God's way works!

> ### "REAL-LIFE RESULTS FROM CFC COUNSELEES"
> #### OBEYING GOD
> Another couple retired a $22,000 debt in four years beating their five-year goal. They were able to live on his income alone and the wife stayed at home and home schooled two children. They bought a used car and paid off a 36-month loan in 20 months. Now they are able to tithe and to give to other ministries. They bought a house and paid the mortgage off in nine years. God's way works!

How to Make the Right Decision Every Time

In Proverbs 2:1–2 (TLB), God says, *"Every young man who listens to me and obeys my instructions will be given wisdom and good sense."* We derive two key questions from these verses. (1) "God, what are You telling us? We're listening." (2) "What do You want us to do about it? You want us to obey Your instructions."

If we listen and obey, wisdom and good sense will be given to us, and most of financing is a matter of wisdom and good sense. God goes on to say, in verses 3 through 5, *"Yes, if you want better insight [a better understanding of God's Word] and discernment [to know right from wrong], and are searching for them as you would for lost money or hidden treasure, then wisdom will be given you."* We need to want insight and discernment; God will not force them on us. We need to be searching for insight in His Word. He is not going to drop a spiritual rock on our head and grant us all wisdom overnight. If we are searching for it and if we want it, wisdom and knowledge of God will be given to us.

We will get to know God for who He is—the almighty, all-merciful, all-forgiving, all-loving God. And when we get to know Him for who He is, something will soon happen: *"You will soon learn the importance of reverence for the Lord and of trusting him"* (Proverbs 2:5 TLB). When we study God's Word and get to know Him better, we will gain trust and respect and reverence for God. Verse 6 adds, *"For the LORD grants wisdom!"* Wisdom comes from God. *"His every word [the Bible] is a treasure of knowledge and understanding. He grants good sense to the godly—his saints. He is their shield, protecting them and guarding their pathway. He shows how to distinguish right from wrong, how to find the right decision every time. For wisdom and truth will enter the very center of your being, filling your life with joy"* (vv. 6–10). **In these ten verses, God is saying that if we will just listen to what He is saying and do what He asks us to do, and if we will search for His wisdom in the Word and desire it, He will reveal to us the wisdom to make the right decision every time. The bottom line is that our lives will be filled with joy, because the greatest blessing Christians can experience is to be obedient to God and have their lives filled with the joy of the Lord.**

PART 2: BUDGET DEVELOPMENT

CHAPTER 4
GET THE FACTS (FORMS 1, 2, AND 3)

Average Monthly Income and Outgo for the Past Calendar Year (Form 1)

The purpose of Form 1 is to gather facts from the **past twelve-month calendar year** so that you can have a base on which to project your future budget. God told us in Proverbs 18:13 (TLB), *"What a shame—yes, how stupid!—to decide before knowing the facts!"* This step is simple obedience to God, recording the past so you can know the facts. Then you can decide what is God's best in planning your future budget. Completing Form 1 is most important, even if your past circumstances or income is not the same as your future circumstances or income.

Instructions

Use pencil. Use any records available to arrive at the most accurate figures. **Round all figures off to the nearest dollar** (e.g., $941.36 should be written as $941). **Convert all figures to monthly amounts.** For example, $100/week x 52 weeks/year = $5,200/year ÷ 12 months = $433/month. Fill in every blank. If you do not have an income or expense (outgo) in any item, simply insert a dash (—). If self-employed, do not include business income or expenses on this form; use only the net profit and wages received from your business that were brought home for family as your family gross income. Include all income from any source, and include all expenses for any reason. Do not list any item more than one place, but include every dollar somewhere. If you can't find a listing on Form 1 for one of your sources of income or outgo, then write in the item under the Other category. Remember to write in the average monthly income and outgo for each item (e.g., for the electric bill average, add up all the electric bills you paid in the past calendar year and divide that total by 12 months to determine the accurate monthly average). If you pay for most items by check and you have your checks returned by the bank, simply make a separate pile of checks for each category—telephone, water, food, clothing—then total each pile and divide by 12.

This exercise will not include the items that you paid for in cash, so you need to estimate all cash expenditures. If you do not have a record for an item, such as eating out, estimate the amount per week (as expenditures can more accurately be recalled in weekly time periods); then convert it to a monthly figure as shown above. Do not go back and change any figures except to correct errors or oversights. Do not try to balance the income with the expenses by changing figures. Simply record all items as accurately as possible and let the difference remain as it is. The smaller the difference is, the better record keeper you are.

AVERAGE MONTHLY INCOME AND OUTGO FOR THE PAST CALENDAR YEAR

FROM Jan 1, 08 TO Dec 31, 08

	PAST	PROJECTED
GROSS INCOME PER MONTH	3,000	
Salary, Pension, Soc Sec (His)	1,733	
Salary, Pension, Soc Sec (Hers)	1,040	
Interest and dividends	5	
Net from Investments/Rents	—	
Gifts and Inheritance	50	
Tax Refunds	72	
Other LOAN	100	

OUTGO PER MONTH

	PAST	PROJECTED
1. Tithe and Offering	90	
2. Taxes (IRS - Soc. Sec.-Med.)	444	
NET SPENDABLE INCOME (GROSS INCOME MINUS LINES 1 & 2) ALSO LIST ON LINE A BELOW	2,466	
3. Housing	1,068	
Mortgage (Rent)	621	
House Insurance	32	
Real Estate Taxes	78	
Electricity / Gas / Oil	107	
Telephone	62	
Water & Sewage	54	
Trash Removal	18	
Maintenance	41	
Cable TV	23	
Other FURNITURE	32	
4. Food (Grocery Store)	269	
5. Auto (Transportation)	487	
Payments	288	
Gas	96	
Auto Insurance	48	
License Tag	3	
Repairs / Maintenance	52	
Vehicle Replacement	—	
6. Insurance	324	
Life	22	
Health	291	
Other DISABILITY	11	

	PAST	PROJECTED
7. DEBTS	333	✳
Credit Cards	268	
Installment Loans	40	
Other UNCLE BEN	25	
8. Enter/Recreation	173	
Dining Out	45	
Trips / Vacation	58	
Babysitters	18	
Activities	26	
Video Rentals	8	
Other BOAT	18	
9. Clothing (Cash)	42	
10. Savings (+or-)	-74	✳
11. Investments (+or-)	—	✳
12. Medical Expenses	87	
Doctor	56	
Dentist	12	
Prescriptions	7	
Other GLASSES	12	
13. Miscellaneous	367	
Drugstore Items	21	
Beauty / Barber	22	
Laundry / Dry Cleaning	5	
Lunch (Work / School)	64	
Subscriptions	9	
Gifts (Incl Christmas)	58	
Special Education	—	
Pocket Money	43	
Pet Store / Veterinarian	11	
Other CHILD CARE	134	
TOTAL EXPENSES (3-13) (ALSO LIST ON LINE B BELOW)	3,076	
A. NET SPENDABLE INCOME	2,466	
B. LESS EXPENSES (3-13)	3,076	
C. DIFFERENCE/MONTH (+OR-) (LINE A MINUS LINE B)	-610	
D. DIFFERENCE/YEAR (+OR-) (MULTIPLY LINE C X 12)	-7,320	

INSTRUCTIONS

Insert only "Past" income and outgo on the lines—after chapter 7 insert only "Projected" income and outgo in the boxes.

Use pencil—use the most accurate figures possible. Fill every blank; if no amount, insert a dash (—).

Round all figures off to the nearest dollar (for example, 941.36 should be 941, and 941.82 should be 942).

Convert all weekly figures to monthly (for example, $100/week x 52 weeks = $5,200/year ÷ 12 months = $433/month).

If self-employed do NOT include business income and use only your net profit from the business that was brought home for the family's use.

✳ Do these 3 projections last and divide your abundance among them only when planning your budget projections.

FORM #1

How to Determine Your Gross Income per Month (All Money Coming In)

For all salaried persons, we do not use take-home pay, only gross income. Payroll deductions, such as insurance, credit union savings, debt payments, bonds, union dues, and so forth, should be listed in the appropriate expense category, described later in this chapter. List all gross income per month. Gross income is the amount earned before any deductions, such as taxes, Social Security, hospitalization premiums, and the like, are made. Be sure to include commissions, bonuses, fees, tips, pensions, and Social Security received. Also include other income, such as gifts, inheritance, child support, alimony, and loans. Other income should include money received from the sale of cars, boats, and other items.

Investment income should be listed only as net profit or loss (a loss of $120 per month should be listed as a minus: –$120). For multiple investments, combine the results.

Self-employment income should be listed only as a net profit or loss. For a sole proprietor, not incorporated, this would be the net from business that was taken home to provide for the family before paying income taxes.

Retirement income for people who receive pensions or have Social Security incomes should list their gross income before anything is taken out, such as IRS withholding or Medicare premiums. IRS withholdings should be listed under outgo per month, Expense, category 2: Taxes. Medicare premiums deducted from your check should be listed under Expense, category 6: Insurance. After listing all income, add it up and place the total amount in the space to the right of the boldface words **GROSS INCOME PER MONTH**.

How to Determine Your Total Outgo per Month (All Money Going Out)

Use the best records you have to determine the most accurate figures possible. If you keep written records, use them. Some information could be obtained from receipts. Another way—possibly the most accurate way—to determine your outgo over a twelve-month period, is to take all of the checks written in that period and divide them up into separate piles—all electric bills in one pile, all telephone bills in another, etc. When all checks for the twelve-month period are divided, total each pile and divide by 12 to get your average per month. Then record the monthly average on Form 1 in the corresponding category item.

If you do not get your checks back from the bank, you could use another system. Use columnar paper or draw columns on blank paper. Use a separate column for each item, and record all twelve months' expenses for that item in the appropriate column—one column for electric, one for telephone, etc. Then total each column and divide by 12 to get your average amount per month.

Category 1: Tithe and Offerings

The total amount in the Tithe and Offerings category should include all monetary gifts and donations to churches and religious organizations, whether given by check or cash. Do not include noncash donations, as we are dealing with cash flow in budgeting, not tax deductions. All charitable contributions should be listed under the Miscellaneous category of Gifts. Remember to convert your weekly church contributions to a monthly amount. For example, $100/week x 52 ÷ by 12 months/year = $433/month. Do not take $100/week x 4, as that will account for only 48 weeks, not 52 weeks in a year.

Category 2: Taxes

The total amount in the Tax category should include all amounts **paid out in the past twelve-month period. This total would include Federal Income Tax, Social Security, and Medicare amounts withheld or paid, also state, county, or municipal income tax withheld or paid, if applicable**. This category does not include sales tax, real estate taxes, or other type of taxes. These non-withholding taxes are listed elsewhere on the form. An easy way to determine this information is to obtain the withholding taxes from your most recent W-2 forms or your income tax return and add to that amount any other amounts that may have been paid directly to the IRS in that same calendar year. Then divide the total paid by 12 to get your monthly average.

After completing your total gross income, subtract category totals 1 and 2 from the total gross income and record the balance as NET SPENDABLE INCOME.

Category 3: Housing

If you are renting, cross out the word *Mortgage*. If you are buying, cross out the word *Rent*. If you have more than one mortgage, list the second mortgage under *Other*. If your mortgage payment includes *principle*, *interest*, *taxes*, and *insurance*, bracket those words and draw a line to the total payment. If your mortgage payment includes only principle and interest, list your insurance and real estate taxes in the spaces provided. Remember to include special tax assessments and flood insurance if applicable. Add up your past twelve electric bills and divide by 12 to get your average electric expense per month; do the same for gas, water, trash removal, and telephone.

Your average monthly maintenance includes such items for the house as painting, electric, and plumbing repairs, carpet cleaning, bug spraying, lawn care, fertilizer, etc. The Other category includes home improvements and purchases of furniture, appliances, and the like. If furniture and appliances are financed, they should be included under Debts (category 7), not housing. In summary, this category should include all money necessary to pay for and operate the home.

Category 4: Food

The Food category includes all purchases made at the grocery store, including nonfood items and pet food. Also include food items purchased elsewhere, such as at fruit stands and convenience stores, and ready-to-eat foods that are brought home to eat. Do not include eating out or food purchased for lunch at work or school. Eating out while at work or school goes under Miscellaneous, category 13, and eating out for entertainment goes under Entertainment and Recreation, category 8. If you did not keep records, then estimate the amount spent per week and convert that amount to a monthly figure.

Category 5: Transportation

If you have payments on two cars, add another space and list them separately. If you changed cars during the year, add up the total amount paid on each car and divide the annual total by 12 to obtain the average monthly payment. List the total spent monthly for gas for all cars in the space for gas. Compute the total spent for insurance on all cars for the year and divide by 12 months to obtain the average monthly insurance expense. Remember to convert the annual license tag expense to a monthly figure. Auto Maintenance and Repair should include such things as grease, oil changes, tires, batteries, and tune-ups. The Replacement item is to be used only if you replaced or purchased a vehicle in the year for which you are recording this information (the past twelve-month calendar year). Use the amount of cash down payment you paid out, not the sale price of the car, and divide by 12 to get the monthly average.

Category 6: Insurance

The Insurance category includes health, life, and disability insurance, but not home or auto insurance. Remember to include any premiums that are deducted from your paycheck. Include Medicare premiums that are deducted from your Social Security check in this category. Also include any health-care premiums that may be deducted from your pension check.

Category 7: Debts

The Debts category includes all monthly payments you paid in the twelve-month period to meet debts, such as credit cards, personal loans, medical debts, installment loans, and so on. Do not include home mortgages and automobile payments. If you pay your credit card balance in full each month when received, it is not included in this category but should be included in the category appropriate for the items purchased. If you buy gasoline for your auto with a credit card and pay the balance in full every month, the amount paid should be listed under the Auto category for gas. Remember: Never list any one expenditure under two categories. **Every dollar that comes in can only go out one time.**

Category 8: Entertainment and Recreation

The Dining Out item is for entertainment only and does not include eating out while at work or school. Since most people do not keep records of the amounts spent eating out, including tips, we suggest that you estimate the average amount spent per week and convert that amount to a monthly figure: ($____ /week x 52 ÷ 12 = $____ /month). This category also includes trips and vacations as separate items. Trips includes all trips other than vacation. The type of expenses to include in both Trips and Vacations are such things as travel, lodging, food, entertainment, souvenirs, etc. Babysitting does not include child care while a parent works. Child care while a parent works should be listed under Miscellaneous Other as a write-in. Activities includes such things as movies, concerts, club dues, attendance or participation in sports events, and hobby expense. The Other item should be used as a write-in for recreational vehicles, sports equipment, boats, video rentals, and so on.

Category 9: Clothing

List your clothing expense for the year and divide by 12 to get your monthly average. Only include the clothing paid for in cash or charged on a credit card that was paid in full when the first bill for that item was received. All clothing bought on credit that was paid for on the credit installment plan should be listed under Debts, category 7. Shoes and clothing accessories should be included in this category.

Category 10: Savings

The amount you saved in the past year divided by 12 is your average amount saved monthly. The amount you saved should include the interest or dividend earned. Do not include any money you saved in the past year if you withdrew it during the past twelve months. One way to determine your average monthly savings is to write down your beginning savings balance as of the first day of the twelve-month period and then write down your savings balance at the end of the twelve-month period and subtract the difference. The difference divided by 12 is your average monthly increase or decrease. If you experienced a decrease because you drew out more than you added, list it as a negative (–) amount, (–\$1,200/year ÷12 = –\$100/month). If you have a negative amount, remember to subtract it from your total outgo. Do not add it by mistake.

Category 11: Investments

Savings are usually short-term undesignated funds saved; investments are long-term designated funds, such as IRAs, pensions, profit sharing, mutual funds, annuities, stocks, bonds, and real estate. Many people with low incomes may not have any amount in this category. Use the same method as used in Savings to determine your investment increase or decrease for the twelve-month period.

Category 12: Medical Expenses

The Medical Expenses category should include only those medical expenses that you paid out in the past twelve months that were not reimbursed by Medicare or your health insurance provider. Do not include your premium for medical insurance, as it was included under Insurance, category 6. Be sure to include such items as doctor and dentist bills, eye care and glasses, prescription medicine, hospital bills, ambulance, X-rays, and laboratory work. Do not include nonprescription medicine in this category. List it where you bought it—for example, grocery store or drugstore.

Category 13: Miscellaneous

This category includes expenses that do not fit anywhere else. List all drugstore purchases except prescription medicine, which should be listed in category 12. This drugstore item should be all drugstore-type products and all drugstore-type stores. If you sometimes buy food at a drugstore, just leave it under Drugstore. If you buy cosmetics or other drugstore-type items from direct sales companies, you should include them under this Drugstore item.

Allowances for children and lunches at school for children or at work for parents should be included.

Subscriptions for newspapers, magazines, record clubs, and book clubs should be included.

Gifts, including gifts for birthdays, weddings, Christmas and other holidays, cards, stamps, and gifts to charitable organizations should be included.

Education includes courses for adults or children in private schools and colleges, and it includes all expenses including tuition, books, fees, transportation, and uniforms.

Pocket money is the money you put in your pocket at the beginning of the week and is gone at the end of the week. It is spent on miscellaneous items, such as snacks, drinks, mints, parking meters, bridge tolls, and other items not in any other category. Estimate a weekly amount; then convert it to monthly.

Pet store purchases and veterinarian charges should be included here. If your pet food was purchased at the grocery store or drugstore, just leave it in that category.

The Other item includes any item not included elsewhere that you are listing separately as a write-in. Such items may include child care while a parent works, child support paid out, alimony paid, attorney's fees, accounting fees, bank service charges, union dues, loans to others, and so on.

Instructions

Now add the totals of categories 3 through 13 and place the total as Total Expenses. Then bring the same total to line B, the Less Expense line, and subtract it from line A, the Net Spendable Income. The answer should be placed on line C, the Difference line. If the answer is a negative answer—the expenses were greater than the net spendable income—place a minus sign (–) in front of the answer.

Caution: Do not go back and change any figures to try to make the Net Spendable Income balance with the Total Expenses. Only make changes for greater accuracy if you discovered an error in your previous figures. You need to be honest with yourself, so do not make up any amounts to balance your income or outgo.

This form will reveal to you the accuracy of your record keeping and identify where your income came from and where it went. It is simply a one-page history of your past year's family financial activity put into budget form.

Note: Form 1 has two columns. At this time fill in only the PAST calendar year figures in the first column **on the single lines** on a blank form in the back of the book. The forms are perforated so that you can remove one and put it in the front of the book for easy access. Do not write in the boxes marked PROJECTED at this time.

Current Monthly Income and Outgo Daily Record (Form 2)

Instructions

Use a sharp pencil on Form 2, as the boxes are small. **Record every penny daily, just before going to bed**. Couples should select one "record keeper" in the home. The other spouse is the "reporter" and is responsible to report daily to the record keeper, in writing, every penny he or she receives or spends each day, with a note indicating items purchased. The reporter is also responsible to see that the record keeper records all income and expenses each day before going to bed. Use the Income column of Form 2 to record all **GROSS INCOME** from every source. Identify the source of the income in the left margin. Use abbreviations if space is inadequate. See Form 1 for more details to select the proper category in which each item should be listed. The categories to use for recording the items on Form 2 are the same categories as Form 1. Refer to the sample of Form 2 as a guide and/or the written instructions when you are in doubt.

Before Recording Daily Income and Outgo

On the last day of the previous month, or before you record any income or outgo for the current month, count all "cash on hand" in your wallet, your spouse's wallet, and anywhere in the house, garage, car, or barn—any money that you consider cash on hand. Total the cash on hand at the beginning of the month. Round the amount off to the nearest dollar and place that total in the upper left hand corner of your form.

Next, look in your check register (not your bank statement) and determine your checking account balance on the last day of the previous month, before you made a deposit or wrote a check for the current month. Round that total off to the nearest dollar and place that figure in the upper left hand corner of your form. If you have more than one checking account, combine the balances or draw in another line to include both balances.

Do not record any savings account balances on this form.

Do not include any GROSS self-employed figures on this form, only the business net that you bring home to provide for family use.

Days You Have No Income or Outgo to Record

When you have no income or outgo to record, simply place a dash (—) in the Description column on that day before you go to bed. This will help you to insert all figures on the right line for the right day, as we are creatures of habit and usually write on the next blank line. If we failed to place a dash on the line for a day when we had no income or outgo, we may write the current day's figures on yesterday's line.

Identify All Sundays

Another procedure to help you record on the proper line is to draw a triangle in the upper corner on the days of the month that are Sundays. (See sample day column.) We usually remember the day of the week better than the date of the day, and this procedure helps us to record on the correct line. It also helps us to check our tithe given each Sunday.

CURRENT MONTHLY INCOME AND OUTGO RECORD

USE PENCIL — Record every penny _daily_.

Beginning Cash $ 43   Ending Cash $ 86
Beginning Checking $ 942   Ending Checking $ 499

PROJECTED BUDGET →   PROJECTED OUTGO

MONTH	YEAR	DESCRIPTION OF COLUMNS #1–#12	1 TITHE (GOD)	2 TAXES (GOV'T)	3 HOUSING	4 FOOD GROCERY	5 AUTO	6 INSURANCE	7 DEBTS	8 ENTER. REC.	9 CLOTHING	10 SAVINGS	11 INVESTMENTS	12 MEDICAL	13 MISC.	DESCRIPTION OF MISC. ONLY #13
1		MORTGAGE – LIFE INS. – MASTERCARD			73.00			11.59	74.00						4.60	LUNCH AT SCHOOL
2		CHRISTIAN FINANCIAL COUN. – SEARS	15.00								48.11				7.00	HAIR CUT
3		CHRISTIAN RADIO	10.00												12.14	SHOWER GIFT
4		PUBLIX – GAS – VIDEO		I 55.81		58.21	18.00			2.00					.75	COKE
5	Bob 880.00	IRS – SS – HEALTH INS.		S 54.56				134.30				12.00			10.00	BEAUTY PARLOR
6		BABYSITTER – DR. TOOTH		M 12.76						9.00				35.00		
7		CHURCH – DINING OUT	72.00							12.41						
8															4.60	LUNCH AT SCHOOL
9		ELEC – TEL – WATER – VISA		E	105.11				98.00						1.50	TOLL BRIDGE
10		MASTER CARD – DR. JONES		T	62.21				74.00						5.42	LUNCH AT WORK
11		PUBLIX – GAS		W 51.41 / I 34.38		56.11	16.00								11.23	DRUG STORE
12	Sue 560.00	IRS – SS – MED – BALLGAME		S 34.72						7.25		12.00			36.14	K-MART
13		(NONE)		M 8.12												
14		CHURCH	72.00													
15		TRASH – PUBLIX – UNCLE BEN			18.11	11.24			40.00							
16		JC PENNEY									24.12				5.00	DRY CLEANER
17		(NONE)														
18		PUBLIX – GAS		I 55.81		61.71	17.00								4.82	LUNCH AT WORK
19	Bob 880.00	IRS – SS – MED – HEALTH INS		S 54.56				134.30				12.00			4.62	BIRTHDAY CARDS
20		LAWN CARE – GREASE & OIL		M 12.76	24.11		24.00								26.81	BIRTHDAY GIFT
21		CHURCH – DINING OUT	72.00							13.62						
22		ABC MOWER – MED. REIMBURSE							60.00					-40.00	4.60	LUNCH AT SCHOOL
23		2ND NATL – SAVINGS WITHDRAWAL							41.00			-25.00				
24		DR. BUTCHER							10.00						3.86	ICE CREAM CONES
25		PUBLIX – GAS		I 34.38		54.21	21.00								21.14	DRUG STORE
26	Sue 560.00	IRS – SS – MED – BALLGAME		S 34.72						6.40		12.00			4.73	LUNCH AT WORK
27		(NONE)		M 8.12												
28		CHURCH	72.00													
29		PUBLIX – VISA				14.18			49.00						4.60	LUNCH AT SCHOOL
30		(NONE)														
31															134.00	CHILD CARE
TOTAL INCOME 2,880 / 3,865	MONTHLY TOTALS →		313	401	992	256	47	280	446	51	72	23	–	37	312	TOTAL OUTGO #1–#13 3,280

ADD BEGINNING CASH, CHECKS AND TOTAL MONTHLY INCOME ← → PROOF TOTALS →   ADD ENDING CASH, CHECKING, TOTAL OUTGO → 3,865

PROJECTED BUDGET LESS MONTHLY TOTALS

FORM #2

Income Column (Gross Income from All Sources)

List all gross income (including pennies) from all sources in the Income column on the date received. At the end of the month, total this column and round off the total to the nearest dollar.

Daily Income and Outgo is the ONLY place in the entire book where you record pennies.

Date Column (Day, Month, Year)

Insert the current month and year at the head of the Date column. Use one page for each month. When you start keeping daily records in the middle of any month, you have two options: (1) Go back to the first of the month and write in the most accurate figures you can recall from any and all records you have, or (2) start on the day of the month you started keeping accurate records.

Description Column (Categories 1–12 and 13)

After you place all the expense (outgo) amounts (including pennies) in the proper category at the end of the day, record the description or purpose for the expense in the Description column. Use abbreviations, as space is limited. The descriptions should be listed in the same order as the expense (from left to right). Use the Description column on the left for categories 1 through 12, and use the Description column on the right only for miscellaneous items. If you run out of space, simply modify the plan—expand the box or record more details on the back of the form. (See the sample of this form for the example.) Do not use more than one line for a day.

Expense (Outgo) Columns (Categories 1–13)

List every expense including pennies (your outgo) for any and all reasons. Record them only one time every day before you go to bed. Your outgo includes all cash spent, all checks written, all money given, and all deductions from your paycheck, pension, or Social Security, plus all money you put in savings or investments.

The expense (outgo) columns DO NOT include the money you deposit to your checking account or the cash you place in your wallet. Your cash and checking funds will be recorded as outgo only when they are used to pay for an item, gift, investment, etc.

If you use credit cards, do not record your purchase in any expense column when you make the purchase. The time to record it in your expense column is when you pay for it.

Debit Card Purchases. If you use a debit card, you paid for the item at the time of purchase, and the expense does get recorded in the appropriate expense column on the date purchased. (A debit card purchase takes the money out of your account automatically, just like writing a check. You do not get a monthly bill to be paid at a later date.)

Credit Card Payments. Where do you record a credit card payment? Under Debts, column 7, or under Gas, Clothing, Vacation, or whatever you purchased with the credit card. Here is how you determine where it is recorded: If you used a credit card to purchase an item and you paid the bill that included that item in full within the ten to fifteen days allowed (by the stated due date), then you record the purchased item in the appropriate category. You consider it a cash purchase and record it in the proper column for the item purchased—for example, furniture (Column 3—Housing); gasoline (Column 5—Auto); vacation (Column 8—Entertainment/Recreation), and so on.

If you do not pay for the item in full when the bill is first received, and instead you pay for the purchased item in monthly payments (two or more), then you borrowed the money to make the purchase, and that becomes a loan. You now record all payments for that loan in the Debt column (7) as a credit card payment.

Savings Withdrawals. Savings withdrawals should be listed in the Savings column (10) with a minus in front of those amounts that indicate a withdrawal. When this column is totaled, the withdrawals should be subtracted from the deposits for that month and the net total (which could be a plus or minus) entered on the monthly total line. Do not record savings withdrawals as income.

Investment Withdrawals. Investment withdrawals should be listed in the Investment column (11) with a minus in front of the amount withdrawn. When this column is totaled, the withdrawals should be subtracted from the investment additions for that month and the net total (which could be a plus or minus) entered on the monthly total line.

Medical Insurance Refunds and Medical Payments. Treat medical insurance refunds the same as savings withdrawals. Record the medical insurance refund in the Medical column (12) with a minus in front of the refund amount. When the column is totaled, the refunds should be subtracted from the payments for that month and the net total (which could be a plus or minus) entered on the monthly total line. Do not record refunds as income. Simply record them as credits in the appropriate category.

Auto Expense Reimbursements and Auto Expenses. If you use your personal car for business purposes and your employer reimburses you, the reimbursement amount is recorded in the Auto column (5) with a minus in front of the reimbursement. When the column is totaled, the reimbursements should be subtracted from the auto expenses for that month and the net total (which could be a plus or minus) entered on the monthly total line. Do not record reimbursements as income.

Other Expense Reimbursements. If you receive a reimbursement for any reason other than auto, follow the same procedure as an auto expense reimbursement, except record the expense and reimbursement in the appropriate column. If you bought lunch for a client and paid a bridge toll, and you were reimbursed by your employer, both the expenses when you paid for them and the reimbursement when you received it would be entered in the Miscellaneous column (13). The reimbursement would be listed with a minus in front. When the column is totaled, the reimbursements should be subtracted from the expenses for that month and the net total (which could be a plus or minus) entered on the monthly total line. Do not record reimbursements as income.

Miscellaneous Column. If you find that you spend money for two or more miscellaneous items in the same day and you don't have space to list them separately on the line for that day, what do you do? You have some options: expand the box, upward not downward, by using a box or two in the same column, or consolidate all the miscellaneous spending for that one day and place that total in the Miscellaneous column (13). Place the word *Over* in the Miscellaneous Description column for that day and itemize the detailed spending on the reverse side of the form by listing the date, the item, the individual price, and the total for that day.

After Recording All Daily Entries for the Month

On the last day of the month, after you have recorded all income and outgo for that month, count all the cash on hand, round it off to the nearest dollar, and place that total in the upper right hand corner of your form.

Next, determine your checking account balance at the end of the month. Round it off to the nearest dollar and place that total in the upper right hand corner of the form.

Your ending balances for both cash on hand and checking for the current month are the same balances you place in the upper left hand corner of Form 2 for the next month as Beginning Balances.

Monthly Totals

Add the daily entries in each column for the monthly totals. Be sure to round off all totals to the nearest dollar ($.50 or less, drop the cents; $.51 and over, round up to the next dollar).

Next, add the monthly totals for columns 1 through 13 from left to right and place that Total Outgo on the monthly total line in the Miscellaneous Description column. Remember that you need to subtract the refunds, reimbursements, and withdrawals where applicable.

Proof of Accuracy

Add together your beginning cash and beginning checking balances and your Total Monthly Income. Place that total in the lower left hand corner of your form as your proof total.

Next, add the ending cash, ending checking balances, and your total monthly outgo. Place that total in the lower right hand corner of the form as your proof total.

Both proof totals should be the same if all entries were exactly correct. Because you rounded off all totals to the nearest dollar, you could be off by up to $6 and still consider it balanced. If you are within $6, give yourself an A for accuracy. The two proof totals will reveal to you how good a record keeper you are.

List of Debts (Form 3)

Purpose

The purpose of Form 3 is to make visible the nature of your debts, the amount unpaid, the amount past due, the monthly obligations, and the cost to borrow. If any debts are seriously past due, they deserve immediate attention and should be given top priority. If you are past due on any debts, it is a good idea to contact creditors by phone and in writing also, and let them know you are working on a plan to bring their account current as soon as possible. It is not a good idea to make promises to pay amounts by certain dates if you cannot keep your promise. This form will help you organize and analyze all debts as of the day you prepare the list. A "debt" is money you owe that could be paid in full and the debt would not continue or reoccur without action on your part. Rent, utility bills, insurance premiums, etc. are not debts, they are Operating Expenses.

God tells us in Romans 13:8 (KJV), *"Owe no man any thing."* The only way we can owe no man anything is to get out of debt and stay out of debt. When we complete Form 3, our debts will be organized so we can analyze options to get out of debt.

LIST OF DEBTS

as of **Feb 14, 2008**
date prepared

		1 TO WHOM OWED	2 USED FOR WHAT	3 CURRENT UNPAID BALANCE	4 DOLLAR AMOUNT PAST DUE	5 CONTRACT MONTHLY PAYMENT	6 INTEREST RATE (APR)
HOUSING (Primary home only)							
	1	FIRST FEDERAL	FIRST MORTGAGE	49,870	—	621	9.5%
	2						
	3						
HOUSING TOTAL ⟶				49,870	—	621	
AUTO (Do Not Include Business Vehicles)							
	1	FIRST NATIONAL BANK	'90 CHEVROLET	6,912	—	288	12%
	2						
	3						
AUTO TOTAL ⟶				6,912	—	288	
ALL OTHER DEBTS (List from the largest balance down to the smallest balance)							
	1	SECOND NATIONAL BANK	STUDENT LOAN	3,218	—	41	8%
	2	VISA	CLOTHING-TIRES	2,463	196	98	19.6%
	3	MASTER CARD	VACATION- MISC	1,841	148	74	18.0%
	4	AMERICAN EXPRESS	HOUSEHOLD	960	960	—	18.0%
	5	DR. WILL BILL	CHILD'S OPERATION	840	840	—	—
	6	UNCLE BEN	CATCH UP PAYMENTS	625	75	25	—
	7	ABC MOWER	LAWN MOWER	418	—	40	18.0%
	8	DR. BUTCHER	WIFE'S OPERATION	242	10	5	—
	9						
	10						
	11						
	12						
	13						
	14						
	15						
	16						
	17						
	18						
	19						
	20						
	21						
	22						
	23						
	24						
ALL OTHER DEBTS TOTAL ⟶				10,607	2,229	283	

(Do **NOT** include housing and auto total in this total)

INSTRUCTIONS: Use pencil—Round all figures to the nearest dollar.
If self-employed do NOT include business debts.
You should have 3 separate totals for the 3 different categories of debt.

FORM #3

Instructions

Use pencil. Round all figures off to the nearest dollar ($941.36 should be written as $941). Divide debts into one of three categories: (1) Housing (your primary house only), (2) Auto (transportation), (3) All other debts.

Column 1: To Whom Owed

List the name of the bank, finance company, merchant, doctor, hospital, credit card company, or other creditor from whom you borrowed the money. If it is a relative or friend, list that person's name. List All Other Debts from the largest unpaid balance down to the smallest unpaid balance.

Column 2: Used for What

Under Housing list first mortgage, second mortgage, equity line loan, home improvement loan, or the more specific identification, such as room addition or swimming pool.

Under Auto list the year and make of the car, truck, motorcycle, or other vehicle you use as transportation. If the auto is leased, place the word "leased" in the Interest column.

Under All Other Debts list what the money was used for: furniture; appliances; equipment loans; credit cards; student loans; loan consolidations; personal loans from friends, family, employer, bank, finance companies; all medical debts to doctors, hospitals, laboratories, etc. All other types of installment debts.

Column 3: Current Unpaid Balance

List the current unpaid balance as of the date you are completing the form. As instructed in Column 1, the debts listed in the All Other Debts category should start with **the largest balance down to the smallest balance**. If the vehicle is leased, list the balance as the number of payments remaining times the monthly lease amount.

Column 4: Past Due Amount

List the dollar amount that is past due as of the date the form is prepared. If the date of the form is the 12th and you had a payment due on the 10th and it was not paid, it is past due and should be listed in the Past Due column— even if you have a ten-day grace period. It is still two days past the due date. If you do not have an amount past due, place a dash (—) in this column.

Column 5: Monthly Payment

List the contract monthly payment only. Do not list the amount you paid if it was more or less than the contract amount. If you do not have a monthly payment, place a dash (—) in this column.

Column 6: Interest Rate

If your current statement does not have the interest rate annual percentage rate (APR), obtain it from your original note, security agreement, or contract. If your interest rate is adjustable, note near the percent "ADJ" so you know it may change. If adjustable, list the current rate as of the date the form is prepared. If you do not have an interest charge, place a dash (—) in this column. No interest rate is stated on lease payments; however, you can be sure interest is included in the contract.

Debt Examples Not to List

- Rent is not a debt. You can't pay it off.
- Mortgages on rental or investment property do not get listed on Form 3, as this form is for family debt only.
- Vehicles used exclusively for business should not be listed on Form 3.
- Current utility bills are not considered a debt.
- Do not list any debts for a self-employed business, full-time or part-time, on Form 3. A self-employed business includes any endeavor where you work and receive income other than salary, bonus, and tips. You have your own business or you are classified as an independent contractor working for others.

When All Debts Are Listed

Add columns 3, 4, and 5 in each category and place the totals on the total lines in the spaces with the bold lined boxes. If you have debts in all three categories, you should have three separate totals, one for each of the three categories.

After you have developed your new budget, this form will be used to analyze options to get out of debt and stay out of debt. Do not try to do this until you have your new budget completed.

"REAL-LIFE RESULTS FROM CFC COUNSELEES"

DEBT FREE!

My financial situation has changed due to your guidance, time, effort, and much prayer. My creditors have been paid in full. I am tithing again and have been able to put some money into savings. I can't begin to describe the good feelings this has produced.

CHAPTER 5
DEVELOP A GUIDE (FORM 4)

The purpose of Form 4 is to determine what the average family with your level of income is spending in the various categories.

Step 1: Determine Your Projected Gross Annual Income

If your projected annual income is going to be very close to your past annual income, you can use the same gross monthly income as recorded on your Form 1 (times 12 to get your gross annual income). Most individuals and families will have a different income each year due to job changes, salary increases, changed hours, bonuses, commissions, and other factors.

The purpose of this step is to estimate as accurately as possible your realistic projected income. It is better to estimate your income on the lower side so you don't set your budget spending too high. When estimating your projected income, use Form 1 as your worksheet and write in your projections for each source of income in the boxes to the right of each source. (See sample.)

After projecting your gross average monthly income from all sources for the next twelve months on Form 1, transfer that total gross average monthly income to the box on Form 4, line A.

Multiply line A times 12 to determine your gross annual income. Now stop working on Form 4 and complete Step 2.

AVERAGE MONTHLY INCOME AND OUTGO FOR THE PAST CALENDAR YEAR

PAST   PROJECTED   FROM Jan 1, 08 TO Dec 31, 08

	PAST	PROJECTED
GROSS INCOME PER MONTH	3,000	3,130
Salary, Pension, Soc Sec (His)	1,733	1,907
Salary, Pension, Soc Sec (Hers)	1,040	1,213
Interest and dividends	5	10
Net from Investments/Rents	—	—
Gifts and Inheritance	50	—
Tax Refunds	72	—
Other LOAN	100	—

OUTGO PER MONTH

	PAST	
1. Tithe and Offering	90	
2. Taxes (IRS - Soc. Sec.-Med.)	444	
NET SPENDABLE INCOME (GROSS INCOME MINUS LINES 1 & 2) ALSO LIST ON LINE A BELOW	2,466	
3. Housing	1,068	
Mortgage (Rent)	621	
House Insurance	32	
Real Estate Taxes	78	
Electricity / Gas / Oil	107	
Telephone	62	
Water & Sewage	54	
Trash Removal	18	
Maintenance	41	
Cable TV	23	
Other FURNITURE	32	
4. Food (Grocery Store)	269	
5. Auto (Transportation)	487	
Payments	288	
Gas	96	
Auto Insurance	48	
License Tag	3	
Repairs / Maintenance	52	
Vehicle Replacement	—	
6. Insurance	324	
Life	22	
Health	291	
Other DISABILITY	11	

	PAST		
7. DEBTS	333		✷
Credit Cards	268		
Installment Loans	40		
Other UNCLE BEN	25		
8. Enter/Recreation	173		
Dining Out	45		
Trips / Vacation	58		
Babysitters	18		
Activities	26		
Video Rentals	8		
Other BOAT	18		
9. Clothing (Cash)	42		
10. Savings (+or-)	-74		✷
11. Investments (+or-)	—		✷
12. Medical Expenses	87		
Doctor	56		
Dentist	12		
Prescriptions	7		
Other GLASSES	12		
13. Miscellaneous	367		
Drugstore Items	21		
Beauty / Barber	22		
Laundry / Dry Cleaning	5		
Lunch (Work / School)	64		
Subscriptions	9		
Gifts (Incl Christmas)	58		
Special Education	—		
Pocket Money	43		
Pet Store / Veterinarian	11		
Other CHILD CARE	134		

	PAST	
TOTAL EXPENSES (3-13) (ALSO LIST ON LINE B BELOW)	3,076	
A. NET SPENDABLE INCOME	2,466	
B. LESS EXPENSES (3-13)	3,076	
C. DIFFERENCE/MONTH (+OR-) (LINE A MINUS LINE B)	-610	
D. DIFFERENCE/YEAR (+OR-) (MULTIPLY LINE C X 12)	-7,320	

INSTRUCTIONS

Insert only "Past" income and outgo on the lines—after chapter 7 insert only "Projected" income and outgo in the boxes.

Use pencil—use the most accurate figures possible. Fill every blank; if no amount, insert a dash (—).

Round all figures off to the nearest dollar (for example, 941.36 should be 941, and 941.82 should be 942).

Convert all weekly figures to monthly (for example, $100/week x 52 weeks = $5,200/year ÷ 12 months = $433/month).

If self-employed do NOT include business income and use only your net profit from the business that was brought home for the family's use.

  ✷ Do these 3 projections last and divide your abundance among them only when planning your budget projections.

FORM #1

MONTHLY BUDGET GUIDE

Date Completed MARCH 12, 2008

A. PROJECTED GROSS AVERAGE MONTHLY INCOME (from form #1) $ 3,130

B. PROJECTED GROSS ANNUAL INCOME (Line A x 12) $ 37,560

BUDGET CATEGORIES 1.	FROM 2. PERCENTAGE GUIDE	from Line A 3. GROSS MONTHLY INCOME	YOUR 4. GUIDE (nearest dollar)
1. Tithe (God)	10 % X	$ 3,130 =	$ 313
2. Taxes (Gov't)	16 % X	$ 3,130 =	$ 501

C.   TOTAL OF CATEGORIES 1. & 2. = $ 814

D. NET SPENDABLE INCOME (Line A minus Line C) $ 2,316

BUDGET CATEGORIES	FROM PERCENTAGE GUIDE	from Line D NET MONTHLY INCOME	YOUR GUIDE (nearest dollar)
3. Housing	28 % X	$ 2,316 =	$ 648
4. Food	14 % X	$ 2,316 =	$ 324
5. Auto	12 % X	$ 2,316 =	$ 278
6. Insurance	6 % X	$ 2,316 =	$ 139
7. Debts	5 % X	$ 2,316 =	$ 116
8. Enter/Recreation	6 % X	$ 2,316 =	$ 139
9. Clothing	5 % X	$ 2,316 =	$ 116
10. Savings	5 % X	$ 2,316 =	$ 116
11. Investment	8 % X	$ 2,316 =	$ 185
12. Medical	4 % X	$ 2,316 =	$ 93
13. Miscellaneous	7 % X	$ 2,316 =	$ 162

E. NET SPENDABLE TOTAL (Total of Categories 3-13, should equal line D.) $ 2,316

INSTRUCTIONS:
Use pencil. Use nearest dollar amount. Use **gross monthly income** in column 3 for categories 1 & 2.
Use **net spendable income** in column 3 for categories 3-13. Gross incomes below $30,000 do **NOT**
have a percentage in the investment category. Use the best estimate for your projected
gross average monthly income on Line A. This is NOT YOUR budget, or your limit, only a
guide for your income level. DO NOT change any percent from the guide.

FORM #4

PERCENTAGE GUIDE FOR FAMILY INCOME

FAMILY OF FOUR

(The Net Spendable percentages also are applicable to "Head of Household" families of three)

GROSS HOUSEHOLD INCOME	$25,000 or less	$35,000	$45,000	$55,000	$65,000	$85,000	$115,000
1. Tithe	10%	10%	10%	10%	10%	10%	10%
2. *Tax - Married/Head of Household	10%	12%	15%	16%	17%	21%	23%
*Tax - Single/No Dependents	17%	18%	22%	24%	26%	28%	29%
NET SPENDABLE INCOME - Married/HOH	$20,000	$27,300	$33,750	$40,700	$47,450	$58,650	$77,050
Single	$18,250	$25,200	$30,600	$36,300	$41,600	$52,700	$70,150
3. Housing	38%	36%	32%	30%	30%	30%	29%
4. Food	14%	12%	13%	12%	11%	11%	11%
5. Auto	14%	12%	13%	14%	14%	13%	13%
6. Insurance	5%	5%	5%	5%	5%	5%	5%
7. Debts	5%	5%	5%	5%	5%	5%	5%
8. Entertainment	4%	6%	6%	7%	7%	7%	8%
9. Clothing	5%	5%	5%	6%	6%	7%	7%
10. Savings	5%	5%	5%	5%	5%	5%	5%
11. Investment	----	5%	5%	5%	5%	5%	5%
12. Medical	5%	4%	4%	4%	4%	4%	4%
13. Miscellaneous	5%	5%	7%	7%	8%	8%	8%

* - For all self-employed persons add 7.65% of Gross Income for Self-Employment Tax

 CHART 5.1

Step 2: Select Your Percentage Guide

Turn to Chart 5.1, Percentage Guide, for various levels of income. Select the income level that is the closest to your projected gross annual income from Form 4, line B. Mark an X on Chart 5.1 above the level you selected. Then transfer all percentages in your income level from the guide to Form 4, column 2. For incomes less than $25,000, use the $25,000-level percentages. For incomes over $115,000, use the $115,000-level percentages. If your income is exactly in the middle of two levels, use the level above or below—the one you feel may be more correct if circumstances change for any reason. Do not change any percentages in the guide except for singles without dependents in category 2, Taxes. Singles without dependents use the percentages on the singles line for their Tax Guide. All others use the category 2 tax percentage on the married/head of household line. Do not omit a category just because you don't have any money spent in that category. If you do not have any money spent on Debts (category 7), do not omit the percent for that category nor transfer that percent to another category.

This is only a guide for families with your income level. **It is not your budget, not your limit, but simply a guide to help you identify any of your excess spending or underspending as compared with the average family.** You will note that the $25,000-level income does not have any percentage for Investment (category 11). That is because the average family with that income level is not investing; usually it takes all their income to provide for their present needs. This does not mean that families in that income level could not or should not allocate funds for investments.

You will also note that category 1, Tithe (God), is 10 percent for all levels of income. While all other percentages are based on the average family, the average family is not giving God 10 percent of their gross income. So we use the Bible, "God's book of finance," to obtain our 10 percent minimum percentage guide.

These percentages are based on the average family of four persons. Do not change any percentages on the guide just because you are a family of one or twelve. Your adjustments will be made on Form 5, column 5, which is your Budget Analysis, where you will later record your budget.

The percentage in categories 1 and 2, God and Government, are based on gross income from all sources. The percentage in categories 3 through 13 total 100 percent of Net Spendable and are based on the Net Spendable amount.

Step 3: Determine the Guideline Amounts for Your Income Level

After you have transferred all the percentages from your income level column of the Chart 5.1 percentage guide to your Form 4, column 2, Monthly Budget Guide, calculate the guideline dollar amounts for your gross income. Insert your gross monthly income from line A of Form 4 to column 3, categories 1 and 2, as that is your multiplier for those two categories only. Next, multiply the Tithe (God) percent in column 2 times your multiplier in column 3, and place the answer in column 4 on the same line. Remember to round off all figures to the nearest dollar ($.50 and less is dropped; $.51 and more is rounded off to the next highest dollar). Then complete category 2, Taxes (Government), in the same manner. When both categories 1 and 2 are complete, add them up and place the total on line C, column 4.

Next, subtract line C from line A (Gross Monthly Income). The difference is your Net Spendable guideline income and is placed on line D in the box. Before you proceed, double-check your math up to this point, because this Net Spendable amount is your multiplier for categories 3 through 13, and if it is wrong, all the remaining answers will be wrong. To proof your work, recalculate all your figures, add line D and line C, and your answer should be line A.

Now use line D (Net Spendable Income) as your multiplier for categories 3 through 13, and insert that amount in column 3 for each of the remaining categories. Next, multiply the percentage in column 2, category 3 (Housing), times the multiplier, column 3 (Net Spendable Income), and record your answer on the same line column 4 guide. Remember to round off all your answers to the nearest dollar in column 4.

Now complete categories 4 through 13 in the same manner. When all categories are completed, add column 4, categories 3 through 13, and place your answer on line E in the box.

Line E, Net Spendable Total, should be the same as line D, Net Spendable Income. If they are not the same but they are $1, $2, or $3 over or under, it is probably due to the rounding-off process. If that is the case, you need to force a balance. If line E is $2 over your line D, then subtract $1 from any two categories from 3 through 13 to force line E to equal line D. If line E is $1 under your line D, then add $1 to any of the categories 3 through 13 to force line E to equal line D. If your line E is $4 or more over or under, you probably made an error in your multiplication or in recording the correct percentage in column 2. A double check of percentages could be made from the percentage guide. If you add the percentages in column 2, categories 3 through 13, they should equal 100 percent. You are now ready to proceed to your Budget Analysis, Form 5.

"REAL-LIFE RESULTS FROM CFC COUNSELEES"

ATTITUDE

My wife and I wish we had received your Godly counsel thirty years ago, we both have changed attitudes. Working together we have decreased our debt by $13,000 in just two months.

CHAPTER 6
ANALYZE YOUR INCOME
AND OUTGO (FORM 5)

The purpose of Form 5 is to analyze how your past budget compares with the guide for your level of income in each category so you can identify the problem areas. You cannot solve any problem until you identify it. Column 3 of Form 5 helps you identify your problem categories for your level of income.

After you analyze how you compare and identify your problem categories, you then have the facts to plan a better-balanced budget for the future months and years.

Step 1: List Your Past Budget Totals
Transfer all your totals from Form 1 (Past Monthly Budget recorded on the lines) to Form 5, column 1.

Step 2: List Your Projected Budget Guide
Transfer all your totals from Form 4 (Monthly Budget Guide, column 4 and lines A, D, and E) to Form 5, column 2.

Step 3: List the Differences
Subtract column 2 from column 1 in each category and record the difference in column 3. If column 2 is less than column 1, the difference in column 3 will be a positive (+), and if column 2 is greater than column 1, the difference in column 3 will be a negative (–). A plus sign (+) will indicate that your past spending or allocation for that category is greater than the guide. A minus sign (–) will indicate that your past spending or allocation for that category is less than the guide.

A plus sign usually means bad news, categories where you are spending or allocating too much. However, if you have a negative in categories 1, 10, or 11, that is bad news, indicating that you are undergiving to God, undersaving, or underinvesting for your level of income.

BUDGET ANALYSIS

Date Completed __MARCH 12, 2008__

COLUMN	1 PAST MONTHLY BUDGET (FROM FORM #1)	2 MONTHLY BUDGET GUIDE (FROM FORM #4)	3 DIFFERENCE (SUBTRACT COLUMN 2 FROM COLUMN 1) + IF OVER GUIDE – IF UNDER GUIDE	4 order of difference	5 PROJECTED MONTHLY BUDGET
A. GROSS MONTHLY INCOME	$ 3,000	$ 3,130			$
1. TITHE (God) (OFFERINGS)	90	313	– 223	2	
2. TAXES (Gov't) (IRS - SS - MED)	444	501	– 57	10	
B. NET SPENDABLE INCOME (GROSS MINUS CATEGORIES 1 & 2)	$ 2,466	$ 2,316			$
3. HOUSING	1,068	648	+ 420	1	
4. FOOD	269	324	– 55	11	
5. AUTO	487	278	+ 209	4	
6. INSURANCE	324	139	+ 185	7	
7. DEBTS	333	116	+ 217	3	
8. ENTER/RECREATION	173	139	+ 34	12	
9. CLOTHING	42	116	– 74	9	
10. SAVINGS	– 74	116	– 190	6	
11. INVESTMENTS	—	185	– 185	8	
12. MEDICAL	87	93	– 6	13	
13. MISCELLANEOUS	367	162	+ 205	5	
C. TOTALS (3-13 only)	$ 3,076	$ 2,316			$
DIFFERENCE (B minus C)	$ – 610				

INSTRUCTIONS:

Use pencil. Use nearest dollar amount. Complete column #1 from form #1, column #2 from form #4, and place the difference in column #3. To complete column #4 disregard the (+) and (–) in column #3 and number the differences from the largest difference #1 to the smallest difference #13, **DO NOT** complete column #5 until you have read chapter 7 and completed your new projected budget in the boxes on form #1. When your new projected budget is completed on form #1 then transfer your figures from form #1 to column #5, Form #5 above.

FORM #5

Step 4: Identify Your Largest to Smallest Differences

Disregard the plus and minus signs in column 3 and number the differences in column 4, rating from the largest difference (1) to the smallest difference (13). If you have two categories with the same difference (e.g., $91) and your next number to list is 5, number the first $91 as 5 and the second $91 as 6.

Column 4 will identify the categories with the biggest differences, either over or under, so you can start your corrections in those categories with the biggest differences first.

Usually, the four biggest problem categories are:

- Category 3. Housing (usually overspending)
- Category 5. Auto (usually overspending)
- Category 7. Debts (usually overspending)
- Category 10. Savings (unable to save because of overspending)

We overspend and overborrow for housing; we overspend and overborrow for autos; and we overspend and overborrow for all other items that are financed or bought on credit cards. Then we are not able to save, so we undersave for our income. Categories 3, 5, and 7 are directly debt related, and category 10 is indirectly debt related. Excessive debt prevents us from being able to save.

God tells us in Proverbs 21:20 (TLB), *"The wise man saves for the future, but the foolish man spends whatever he gets."* He is telling us to spend less and save more. **Overspending for one's level of income is one of the greatest budget problems.**

Step 5. Identify Your Problem Areas

Analyze every category on Form 5: Budget Analysis; identify your problem areas, consider all the options you have to improve the balance between your income and outgo, and take action to be a better manager of what God has entrusted to you.

Do not complete Form 5, column 5 at this time. You do not pick a figure out of the air and place it in column 5. If you do not know how the reduction is going to happen, it won't happen. You need to develop your new budget category by category, item by item, after prayerfully researching hints and ideas to improve and after prayerfully adopting the proper attitude, which is, *I sincerely desire to improve.*

Chapter 7 will guide you through the steps to develop your new, better, and balanced budget. As you proceed through chapter 7, the amounts needed for Form 5, column 5, will be determined.

"REAL-LIFE RESULTS FROM CFC COUNSELEES"
MORTGAGE PRE-PAYMENT

My husband and I greatly appreciate your help. As of this writing, we have made additional principal payments on our mortgage, which has resulted in an interest savings of $46,176. With the Lord's help, I believe that we will have this thirty-year mortgage paid in full within ten years. Thank you for your guidance.

CHAPTER 7
DEVELOP A BALANCED BUDGET

Step 1: Make a List of Ways to Improve

Before completing column 5 of Form 5, **read the Cost-Cutting Hints in appendix A (pages 101–110)**. Check off all the ideas you are going to try now, and estimate how much you will save per month. Place the amount you will save on the Cost-Cutting List to the left of each idea you are going to start now. Do not check off the items that you are already doing. You only want to know how much you are going to save in the future. You can add your own ideas to the Cost-Cutting Hints and indicate how much they will save you. This list is not complete, nor does it include every idea for every budget; it is only a list to stimulate your thoughts on ways to cut future costs.

Step 2: Start Your New Projected Monthly Budget

Go back to your Form 1 (Average Monthly Income and Outgo) and use it as a worksheet for your projected budget in the months ahead. All projected estimates should be placed in the second column of figures in the boxes. You should have completed the projections for Future Income on Form 1 before doing your Form 4. Now complete all the projection estimates for your Future Outgo. Use the insight obtained from the overspending items on Form 5 as you proceed with developing your budget in this chapter.

Step 3: Time for an Attitude Adjustment?

Before you begin, you need to remember that we don't have money problems—we have attitude problems about money matters. **Our first attitude change should be: CAN I/WE IMPROVE?** You should ask this question as you analyze each item of your outgo. If your budget does not balance the first time after you have completed your future projections on Form 1, then it is time to adopt another attitude. **Second Attitude Change: IS THIS ITEM A NEED, A WANT, OR A DESIRE?** If the item is not a need, you could cut back or cut out the item from your future budget. Again, ask yourself the question as you analyze each item. If the budget does not balance the second time you go through your complete outgo on Form 1 as a worksheet, you get a third chance, just as in baseball.

Before you go through the third time, you need another attitude adjustment. You need to remember the sign in the remote hunting camp:

> **If there is anything that you need
> And you can't find it,
> Just let us know,
> And we'll show you
> How to get along without it!**

You need to prayerfully adopt the attitude that asks, **"CAN I/WE MAKE DO OR DO WITHOUT?"** Ask yourself this question as you analyze each item. Some of you will have balanced your budget the first time, others the second or third time. If you were serious about improving and cut back or cut out each of the three times and you still don't have a balanced budget, we will assume you did everything you could to reduce your future outgo by this method.

AVERAGE MONTHLY INCOME AND OUTGO FOR THE PAST CALENDAR YEAR

FROM Jan 1, 08 TO Dec 31, 08

	PAST	PROJECTED
GROSS INCOME PER MONTH	3,000	3,130
Salary, Pension, Soc Sec (His)	1,733	1,907
Salary, Pension, Soc Sec (Hers)	1,040	1,213
Interest and dividends	5	10
Net from Investments/Rents	—	
Gifts and Inheritance	50	—
Tax Refunds	72	—
Other LOAN	100	—
OUTGO PER MONTH		
1. Tithe and Offering	90	313
2. Taxes (IRS - Soc. Sec.-Med.)	444	437
NET SPENDABLE INCOME (GROSS INCOME MINUS LINES 1 & 2) ALSO LIST ON LINE A BELOW)	2,466	2,380
3. Housing	1,068	770
Mortgage (Rent)	621	421
House Insurance	32	28
Real Estate Taxes	78	80
Electricity / Gas / Oil	107	97
Telephone	62	36
Water & Sewage	54	54
Trash Removal	18	18
Maintenance	41	36
Cable TV	23	—
Other FURNITURE	32	—
4. Food (Grocery Store)	269	238
5. Auto (Transportation)	487	160
Payments	288	—
Gas	96	84
Auto Insurance	48	37
License Tag	3	3
Repairs / Maintenance	52	36
Vehicle Replacement	—	—
6. Insurance	324	313
Life	22	22
Health	291	291
Other DISABILITY	11	—

	PAST	PROJECTED
7. DEBTS	333	427 ✱
Credit Cards	268	327
Installment Loans	40	60
Other UNCLE BEN	25	40
8. Enter/Recreation	173	100
Dining Out	45	20
Trips / Vacation	58	54
Babysitters	18	9
Activities	26	13
Video Rentals	8	4
Other BOAT	18	—
9. Clothing (Cash)	42	32
10. Savings (+or-)	-74	54 ✱
11. Investments (+or-)	—	— ✱
12. Medical Expenses	87	35
Doctor	56	21
Dentist	12	10
Prescriptions	7	4
Other GLASSES	12	—
13. Miscellaneous	367	251
Drugstore Items	21	16
Beauty / Barber	22	12
Laundry / Dry Cleaning	5	5
Lunch (Work / School)	64	32
Subscriptions	9	—
Gifts (Incl Christmas)	58	30
Special Education	—	—
Pocket Money	43	22
Pet Store / Veterinarian	11	—
Other CHILD CARE	134	134
TOTAL EXPENSES (3-13) (ALSO LIST ON LINE B BELOW)	3,076	2,380
A. NET SPENDABLE INCOME	2,466	2,380
B. LESS EXPENSES (3-13)	3,076	2,380
C. DIFFERENCE/MONTH (+OR-) (LINE A MINUS LINE B)	-610	—
D. DIFFERENCE/YEAR (+OR-) (MULTIPLY LINE C X 12)	-7,320	

INSTRUCTIONS

Insert only "Past" income and outgo on the lines—after chapter 7 insert only "Projected" income and outgo in the boxes.

Use pencil—use the most accurate figures possible. Fill every blank; if no amount, insert a dash (—).

Round all figures off to the nearest dollar (for example, 941.36 should be 941, and 941.82 should be 942).

Convert all weekly figures to monthly (for example, $100/week x 52 weeks = $5,200/year ÷ 12 months = $433/month).

If self-employed do NOT include business income and use only your net profit from the business that was brought home for the family's use.

✱ Do these 3 projections last and divide your abundance among them only when planning your budget projections.

FORM #1

Step 4: Now It Is Time for Action

Now that our attitude is what God wants it to be, we can begin to prepare our new outgo for the future on Form 1 in the boxes provided. Remember to use pencil so you can revise as needed. Project your future allocations for each item in each category. Every box should have a figure in it, unless you do not plan to allocate any money for that item in the future. Complete categories 1 through 13, except 7 (Debts), 10 (Savings), and 11 (Investments). The asterisk at the bottom of the form is your reminder to leave these three items for last, until you know how much is in your abundance. When you have completed all the boxes the first time (except 7, 10, and 11), subtract 1 and 2 (Tithes and Taxes) from your Projected Gross Monthly Income to determine your Projected Net Spendable Income. Now add up your projected outgo of items 3 through 13 (except 7, 10, and 11). Then subtract that total from your Projected Net Spendable Income. The balance is the abundance in your budget that you can allocate toward 7 (Debts) if you have any, and 10 (Savings), and 11 (Investments). The minimum amount needed for 7 (Debts) from your Abundance can be obtained from your Form 3, column 5 (All Other Debts total). The next category to allocate from your Abundance is 10 (Savings). Every person should have some amount to allocate for savings. As we have learned, *"The wise man saves for the future, but the foolish man spends whatever he gets"* (Proverbs 21:20 TLB). We don't want to go through all the work to establish a budget only to be "foolish." The third category to allocate from your Abundance is 11 (Investments). Not everyone, especially those with low incomes, will be able to allocate an amount toward Projected Investments. I do not recommend that you allocate money for Investments if you are heavy in debt with little or no savings. Sometimes the best investment is getting out of debt, especially if you are paying high interest rates on any loans or credit cards.

Proverbs 3:27–28 (TLB) tells us, *"Don't withhold payment of your debts. Don't say 'some other time,' if you can pay now."* God wants you to get out of debt and pay now if you can.

Step 5: Transfer Your New Projected Monthly Budget

When all boxes are complete on Form 1 for your projected budget (even if it is not balanced), transfer all your category totals to Form 5 (Budget Analysis), column 5. Now compare your Form 5, column 2 (Monthly Budget Guide), with your new Projected Monthly Budget in column 5 to see how close you are to the guide. Next, compare your Form 5, column 1 (Past Monthly Budget) with column 5, your new Projected Monthly Budget, to see how you improved over your old budget.

BUDGET ANALYSIS

Date Completed __MARCH 12, 2008__

COLUMN	1 PAST MONTHLY BUDGET (FROM FORM #1)	2 MONTHLY BUDGET GUIDE (FROM FORM #4)	3 DIFFERENCE (SUBTRACT COLUMN 2 FROM COLUMN 1) + IF OVER GUIDE − IF UNDER GUIDE	4 order of difference	5 PROJECTED MONTHLY BUDGET
A. GROSS MONTHLY INCOME	$ 3,000	$ 3,130			$ 3,130
1. TITHE (God) (OFFERINGS)	90	313	− 223	2	313
2. TAXES (Gov't) (IRS - SS - MED)	444	501	− 57	10	437
B. NET SPENDABLE INCOME (GROSS MINUS CATEGORIES 1 & 2)	$ 2,466	$ 2,316			$ 2,380
3. HOUSING	1,068	648	+ 420	1	770
4. FOOD	269	324	− 55	11	238
5. AUTO	487	278	+ 209	4	160
6. INSURANCE	324	139	+ 185	7	313
7. DEBTS	333	116	+ 217	3	427
8. ENTER/RECREATION	173	139	+ 34	12	100
9. CLOTHING	42	116	− 74	9	32
10. SAVINGS	− 74	116	− 190	6	54
11. INVESTMENTS	—	185	− 185	8	—
12. MEDICAL	87	93	− 6	13	35
13. MISCELLANEOUS	367	162	+ 205	5	251
C. TOTALS (3-13 only)	$ 3,076	$ 2,316			$ 2,380
DIFFERENCE (B minus C)	$ − 610				

INSTRUCTIONS:

Use pencil. Use nearest dollar amount. Complete column #1 from form #1, column #2 from form #4, and place the difference in column #3. To complete column #4 disregard the (+) and (−) in column #3 and number the differences from the largest difference #1 to the smallest difference #13, **DO NOT** complete column #5 until you have read chapter 7 and completed your new projected budget in the boxes on form #1. When your new projected budget is completed on form #1 then transfer your figures from form #1 to column #5, Form #5 above.

FORM #5

Summary

If you did your best to improve, you should have found an abundance in your budget and now have a balanced budget, giving you greater peace, joy, and contentment about your finances. Now you have taken that first giant step toward total debt freedom, but **don't give up doing what is right.** *"Let us not get tired of doing what is right, for after a while we will reap a harvest of blessing if we don't get discouraged and give up."* (Galatians 6:9 TLB).

At this point you need to continue keeping up your Form 2 (Daily Record Keeping) and complete the other forms in this book. **Winners never quit; quitters never win.**

Chapter 8 will help you to find an abundance if your budget DID NOT balance in this chapter. You will also learn how to find an even greater abundance in chapter 8 if your budget DID balance.

"REAL-LIFE RESULTS FROM CFC COUNSELEES"
WINNERS NEVER QUIT

Another couple said once is not enough! When they chose NOT to obey God's way the first time they went for counseling their finances grew worse. When they came back the second time several years later their outgo exceeded their income. Their total debt was $112,823 of which $50,594 was consumer debt. In just six months they were on their way to getting out and staying out of debt. They destroyed credit cards, stopped borrowing money, bought only what they needed on a cash basis and started prepaying their house mortgage.

CHAPTER 8
HOW TO ENJOY AN EVEN GREATER ABUNDANCE (FORMS 6, 7, AND 8)

"When your outgo exceeds your income, your upkeep will be your downfall." When your outgo exceeds your income, you have three areas of options to solve your problem. Even when you have a balanced budget and you are not having a budget problem, these three areas of options can help you have greater joy and peace and help you find an even greater abundance in your budget.

Look at it any way you desire—to solve a problem or to find a greater abundance—here are the only three option areas. These three option areas apply to every person, every family, every business, every church, and every government.

- Find options to increase your present income (Form 6).
- Find options to lower existing outgo (Form 7).
- Find options to control your future spending (Form 8).

Now look at the way these three forms work. Pray for God to reveal options to you. Your first column is the date that God revealed the option to you. The second column is the number of options He revealed, and the third column lists each option that God revealed. Please list every option that God reveals, not only the ones that you want to do. List them even if you don't want to do them or will never do them or don't like the option. If it is something that you or anyone in your shoes could do, then list it. God may not reveal every option to you the first day, so keep praying daily for Him to keep on revealing options for you to add to your list.

Column 3 now becomes your prayer list of options you could do. Pray daily, asking God to give you a peace about one or more options on which He wants you to take action. Then list in column 4 (on the same line as that option) the date you took action and in column 5 the action taken and the results you received.

As you listen for options, list them, pray over them for peace, and then act on them and record your responses, you will have visible evidence of how God is directing you and blessing your obedience to His way of managing money. These three option-action forms are simply a tangible way to record your testimony day by day of how God loves you and is blessing you so that you can "enjoy an even greater abundance."

Step 1: Options to Increase Your Present Income (Form 6)
Following is a beginning list of possible options to increase your income. Every item on this list may not be applicable for every person, and each person should add ideas to the list.

OPTIONS TO INCREASE YOUR PRESENT INCOME

DATE [#1]	# [#2]	POSSIBLE OPTIONS [#3]	DATE [#4]	ACTIONS TAKEN AND RESULTS [#5]
3-12	1	SELL EXTRA LAWN MOWER		
3-12	2	ASK FOR OVERTIME WHEN POSSIBLE	3-18	REQUEST MADE— REC'D 4 HRS/WK
3-15	3	SELL GUN COLLECTION		
3-15	4	TAKE A SECOND JOB		
3-16	5	HOLD A GARAGE SALE	3-29	HAD SALE— MADE $621.00
3-18	6	HAVE CHILDREN TAKE P/T JOBS		
	7			
	8			
	9			
	10			
	11			
	12			
	13			
	14			
	15			
	16			
	17			
	18			
	19			
	20			

INSTRUCTIONS: List the date and the possible option on the left side. (List any option that God brings to mind.) Now pray over this list until God gives you a peace about taking action on one or more options then list the date, the action taken, and the results on the right side on the line with the option. Keep adding options day by day as God brings more options to mind, and keep praying over this list daily.

SOME POSSIBLE OPTIONS: Second job, odd jobs, overtime on present job, higher paying position with present employer, different higher paying primary job, spouse take employment, older children take part-time employment, sell assets not needed, hold garage sales, gifts from family, turn hobby into income producer.
PLEASE BE CREATIVE IN PREPARING YOUR LIST.

FORM #6

- The provider could find a second job.
- The provider could work overtime on his or her present job.
- The provider could find odd jobs as available.
- The provider could prepare for a higher-paying job with the same employer.
- The provider could seek a different, higher-paying primary job.
- The spouse, where applicable, could start employment.
- The spouse, where applicable, if already employed, could do the first five items above.
- Older children in the family could take part-time jobs to help the family budget.
- You could sell any assets or items you no longer need.
- You could have a garage or yard sale.
- You could turn a hobby into an income producer.
- You could rent some of your appropriate assets to others.
- You could share your need with a relative who may bless you with a gift.

The purpose of Form 6 is to help you organize, analyze, and compile a list of all the ways you could consider to be a better manager and a better provider for your family and yourself. After you have gathered all the options to increase your income and received counsel from God, the actions He wants you to take usually become obvious.

Every person, regardless of present financial circumstances, should complete these three option-action forms (6, 7, and 8). Completing these forms will give you greater peace, joy, and contentment. Even if you feel you don't need help in this area, you should do it anyway. **God may just have a hidden blessing waiting for your obedience.**

Step 2: Options to Lower Your Existing Outgo (Form 7)

This is a starter list of possible options to reduce your outgo. Again, every item on this list is not for everyone, and each person should add creative ways to the list, as the list is not complete.

- Sell any asset not needed and pay off the debt remaining on that asset.
- Share your housing (rent part) to lower your outgo for the rent or mortgage.
- Prepay part or all of your debts from savings or other assets.
- Ask each creditor to lower your interest rate and monthly payment, if possible, even if it is only for a temporary period of time. Do not be bashful about asking creditors for help; you may be surprised what they offer.
- Reorganize your debts to extend the repayment time and lower your average interest rate and monthly payment.
  - Loan consolidation
  - Equity loan
  - Refinancing of home
- Increase your income and prepay your debts.
- Cut back on your spending and prepay your debts.
- Look for a bank that has low or no service charges for their accounts.

There are some dangers in reorganizing your debts. **Seventy-five percent of those who reorganize their debts with any type of a loan consolidation find themselves right back to the same high payment in only twelve months.** Why? First, because they did not overcome ignorance with wisdom and learn how to manage well. Second, because they did not change their attitude about spending, borrowing, using credit cards, or living within their income. Many times those 75 percent who end up right back where they were with high monthly payments have the wrong attitude: "Now that we have our loan consolidation with lower payments, we can take that luxury vacation or buy that newer car or that big-screen television." When they do such things, the outgo for debt payment goes right back up. The loan consolidation did not solve their problem; it only treated the symptom for twelve months. **More money does not solve our problem if we continue to mismanage when we get more money.**

I encourage you to fix your level of spending below your income level, especially if you consolidate your debts to reduce your outgo. Try to operate on a cash basis from this point on, especially if you consolidated your loans, to prevent your outgo from creeping up above your income again.

OPTIONS TO LOWER YOUR EXISTING OUTGO

DATE #1	#2	POSSIBLE OPTIONS #3	DATE #4	ACTIONS TAKEN AND RESULTS #5
3-12	1	SELL AUTO AND PAY OFF LOAN		
3-12	2	ASK EACH CREDITOR TO LOWER PAYMENTS		
3-12	3	SELL BOAT AND PAY OFF LOAN	3-25	SOLD - LOWERED OUTGO $320/MO.
3-15	4	CONSOLIDATE INSTALLMENT DEBTS		
3-18	5	REFINANCE HOME		
3-18	6	HOME EQUITY LOAN		
	7			
	8			
	9			
	10			
	11			
	12			
	13			
	14			
	15			
	16			
	17			
	18			
	19			
	20			

INSTRUCTIONS: List the date and the possible option on the left side. (List any option that God brings to mind.) Now pray over this list until God gives you a peace about taking action on one or more options then list the date, the action taken, and the results on the right side on the line with the option. Keep adding options day by day as God brings more options to mind, and keep praying over this list daily.

SOME POSSIBLE OPTIONS: Reduce your spending and apply the surplus to your debts; increase your income and apply the surplus to your debts; ask each creditor to lower your monthly payment; sell any asset not needed and on which you are still making payments, then pay off the debt from the proceeds of that sale; loan consolidation or refinancing.
PLEASE BE CREATIVE IN PREPARING YOUR LIST.

FORM #7

Step 3: Options to Control Your Future Spending (Form 8)

We are creatures of habit, and habits are easily formed but hard to break. An extra effort needs to be made to change our poor habits into better habits. Most of our spending is simply a result of our habits—our habitual ways of buying clothes, food, household items, and gifts, for example. **Do we look in the pantry, closet, or garage, make a list of our needs, and buy only those items on our needs list?** Do we make a list of errands to do and then plan the best time and most direct route to save both gasoline and time? Most errands could be planned for one day a week or every two weeks on the way to or from work. If we make a grocery list and shop weekly, we should not run out of needed food items and end up going to the grocery store three to four times a week. What are your spending habits? Could they be improved?

You should be able to fill one or two pages of creative Options to Control Your Future Spending (Form 8). This is the one form of the three option-action forms that counselees fill up first. I have provided a few ways to stimulate your thinking, and you can add to the list as God reveals dozens of more ideas.

- Shop with a need list for food.
- Use coupons only for items on your need list.
- Do not use coupons until you make a price comparison with other brands, especially generic or store brands.
- Shop for price, not labels, in one or more stores.
- When shopping for food, compare fresh, frozen, and canned to determine the best price per serving.
- Shop with a need list for clothing and all other items.
- Avoid carrying or using credit cards for anything.
- Combine errands into a maximum of one trip per week.
- Carry lunch to work and school.
- Eliminate junk food.
- Order only water to drink when eating out.
- Cut back a little in all budget categories.
- Reduce the miles you drive through better planning.
- Reduce the times you turn on electric lights and appliances.
- Use electric fans to allow warmer air-conditioning settings to reduce electric bills.
- Open windows and shut off air-conditioning or heat as weather permits.
- Stay out of stores unless you have an item on your need list.
- Make all future purchases in cash, or pay for higher priced items by check.
- Do not let your mortgage lender retain overages in escrow accounts; ask for refunds.

OPTIONS TO CONTROL YOUR FUTURE SPENDING

DATE [#1]	# [#2]	POSSIBLE OPTIONS [#3]	DATE [#4]	ACTIONS TAKEN AND RESULTS [#5]
3-12	1	SHOP BY "LIST ONLY" FOR FOOD	3-12	STARTED FOOD LIST
3-12	2	USE COUPONS FOR LIST ITEMS ONLY	3-12	STARTED CLIPPING COUPONS
3-12	3	SHOP FOR PRICE, NOT BRAND NAME		
3-15	4	SHOP BY "LIST ONLY" FOR CLOTHING		
3-15	5	CARRY "NO" CREDIT CARDS	3-15	SEALED ALL CARDS IN ENVELOPE
3-18	6	COMBINE ERRANDS INTO 1 TRIP/WEEK		
3-18	7	CARRY LUNCH TO WORK AND SCHOOL	3-20	STARTED PACKING LUNCHES
3-21	8	STOP BUYING JUNK FOOD		
	9			
	10			
	11			
	12			
	13			
	14			
	15			
	16			
	17			
	18			
	19			
	20			

INSTRUCTIONS: List the date and the possible option on the left side. (List any option that God brings to mind.) Now pray over this list until God gives you a peace about taking action on one or more options then list the date, the action taken, and the results on the right side on the line with the option. Keep adding options day by day as God brings more options to mind, and keep praying over this list daily.

SOME POSSIBLE OPTIONS: Shop from a need list only until budget allows for wants and desires; use coupons for items on need list only; prepare need list at home after looking in the pantry, closet and garage; compare prices of other brands before using coupons; cut back in **all** budget categories; shop less frequently and combine your shopping trips; control impulse spending by carrying **NO** credit cards, **NO** checks, and **NO** extra cash, carry **only** the cash needed for that days' planned spending.

PLEASE BE CREATIVE IN PREPARING YOUR LIST.

FORM #8

To be successful in cutting back on all future spending requires the committed faithful support and cooperation of every member in the family. God will bless harmony in the home. **Relationships are more important than money, so be sure you do what you do in love.** Love is the greatest motivator in the world. More important than what we are doing in our planning and spending is why we are doing it. Our purpose for doing anything should be to bring glory to God, to serve others, and to provide for our needs.

Summary

Remember, you can list hundreds of ways to improve, but not one change or improvement is going to take place until you take action to establish a plan and put your plan into action. One secret of success is *Do it now!* Another secret is *Write it down*—a dull pencil is better than a sharp mind.

At this point in your progress, if you have been listening to God and have been obedient to His ways of managing money, you should have found an even greater abundance in your budget and you should have experienced a greater joy and peace.

> ### "REAL-LIFE RESULTS FROM CFC COUNSELEES"
> #### ATITITUDE
> It seemed that everything was against us as we struggled to make our marriage work. We were ready to file bankruptcy when I heard about CFC on the radio. It was recommended that we not file bankruptcy and now just one year later our financial situation is becoming steadily better. The greatest change has been our attitude toward life, God, and each other.

PART 3: BUDGET CONTROL

CHAPTER 9
COMMIT TO FOLLOW THE PLAN (FORM 2)

If we made the best plans anyone ever made to sail to Hawaii but we didn't watch the compass and stay on course, we would never reach our destination, our goal. The same is true with our finances. We can develop an excellent financial plan, but if we don't keep good records and follow the plan (stay on course), we will never reach our goal.

It takes discipline and commitment to reach our goals and become champions, winning the race. Discipline is simply setting the rules. That is, we need to establish a plan (budget) and then make the commitment—a promise or vow—to follow the plan. Sports champions do not win without setting goals (making plans) and then applying the commitment to practice (stay on course) and follow the plan.

The financial plan in this book works if you follow it. As they say in tennis, "The ball is in your court." It is up to you to establish the plan and follow the plan for you and your household.

Step 1: Keep Good Records

After you have completed Forms 1–8, you are now ready to develop your Budget Control system. Remember, you continue to keep your daily income and outgo on Form 2 for every month in the year. You simply take all your completed and future Form 2s and expand their use by adding your new Projected Budget figures in the boxes above each column of Form 2.

It is now time to transfer your Projected Budget figures from Form 5, column 5, to all of your Form 2s in the boxes above each column designated for your projected budget. Next, take all of your completed Form 2s and total each column if you haven't already done so. Remember to round off all totals to the nearest dollar. Now subtract your monthly totals in each column from your Projected Budget totals and record the difference in each column in the bottom line of boxes, Projected Budget Less Monthly Totals. (See the sample on the next page.)

If your monthly total is greater than your Projected Budget total, you have overspent or overallocated for that category that month. When you have overspent, place a circle around the difference. The circle around the difference denotes an *O* for overspent.

If your monthly total is less than your Projected Budget total, you have underspent or underallocated for that category that month. When you have underspent, place a line under the difference. The line under the difference denotes underspending.

Circles around categories 1 (God), 10 (Savings), and 11 (Investments) indicate you overgave, oversaved, or overinvested. Lines under categories 1, 10, and 11 indicate you undergave, undersaved, or underinvested. These three categories are not considered spending categories.

BUDGET CONTROL

CURRENT MONTHLY INCOME AND OUTGO RECORD
USE PENCIL — Record every penny daily.

Beginning Cash $ 43 / Beginning Checking $ 942
Ending Cash $ 86 / Ending Checking $ 499

Beginning Cash 3,130 — Ending Checking 3,130

Day	Description of Columns #1–#12	1 TITHE (GOD) 313	2 TAXES (GOV'T) 437	3 HOUSING 770	4 FOOD GROCERY 238	5 AUTO 160	6 INSURANCE 313	7 DEBTS 427	8 ENTER. REC. 100	9 CLOTHING 32	10 SAVINGS 54	11 INVEST. –	12 MEDICAL 35	13 MISC. 251	Description of Misc. Only #13
1	MORTGAGE – LIFE INS. – MASTERCARD			731⁰⁰			11⁸⁰	74⁰⁰						4⁶²	LUNCH AT SCHOOL
2	CHRISTIAN FINANCIAL COUN. – SEARS	15⁰⁰								48¹¹				7⁰⁰	HAIR CUT
3	CHRISTIAN RADIO	10⁰⁰												12⁴²	SHOWER GIFT
4	PUBLIX – GAS – VIDEO				58²¹	18⁰⁰			2⁰⁰					75	COKE
5	IRS – SS – HEALTH INS.	I 55⁸¹ / S 54⁵⁶					134³⁰				12⁰⁰			10⁰⁰	BEAUTY PARLOR
6	BABYSITTER – DR. TOOTH	M 12⁷⁶							9⁰⁰				35⁰⁰		
7	CHURCH – DINING OUT	72⁰⁰							12⁴¹					4⁶⁰	LUNCH AT SCHOOL
8				E 105¹¹										1⁸⁰	TOLL BRIDGE
9	ELEC – TEL – WATER – VISA			T 62²¹				98⁰⁰						5⁴²	LUNCH AT WORK
10	MASTER CARD – DR. JONES			W 51⁴¹				74⁰⁰					42⁰⁰	11²¹	DRUG STORE
11	PUBLIX – GAS				56¹¹	16⁰⁰								36¹⁴	K-MART
12	IRS – SS – MED – BALLGAME	I 34⁷⁸ / S 34⁷²							7²⁵		12⁰⁰				
13	— (NONE)	M 8¹²													
14	CHURCH	72⁰⁰													
15	TRASH – PUBLIX – UNCLE BEN			18¹¹	11²⁴			40⁰⁰						4⁶⁰	LUNCH AT SCHOOL
16	JCPENNEY									24¹²				5⁰⁰	DRY CLEANER
17	— (NONE)														
18	PUBLIX – GAS				61⁷¹	17⁵⁰								4⁸²	LUNCH AT WORK
19	IRS – SS – MED – HEALTH INS	I 55⁸¹ / S 54⁵⁶					134³⁰				12⁰⁰			4⁶²	BIRTHDAY CARDS
20	LAWN CARE – GREASE & OIL	M 12⁷⁶		24¹¹		24⁹⁰								26⁸¹	BIRTHDAY GIFT
21	CHURCH – DINING OUT	72⁰⁰							13⁶²						
22	ABC MOWER – MED. REIMBURSE							60⁰⁰					40⁰⁰	4⁶⁰	LUNCH AT SCHOOL
23	2ND NATL – SAVINGS WITHDRAWAL							41⁰⁰			25⁰⁰				
24	DR. BUTCHER							10⁰⁰						3⁸⁶	ICE CREAM CONES
25	PUBLIX – GAS				54²¹	21⁰⁰								21¹⁴	DRUG STORE
26	IRS – SS – MED – BALLGAME	I 34³⁸ / S 34⁷²							6⁴²		12⁰⁰			4⁷³	LUNCH AT WORK
27	— (NONE)	M 8¹²													
28	CHURCH	72⁰⁰													
29	PUBLIX – VISA				14¹⁸			49⁰⁰						4⁰⁰	LUNCH AT SCHOOL
30	— (NONE)													134⁰⁰	CHILD CARE
31															

GROSS INCOME ALL SOURCES:
BOB 880⁰⁰ (row 5)
SUE 560⁰⁰ (row 12)
BOB 880⁰⁰ (row 19)
SUE 560⁰⁰ (row 26)

MONTHLY TOTALS → 313 | 401 | 992 | 256 | 97 | 280 | 446 | 51 | 72 | 23 | – | 37 | 312

TOTAL OUTGO #1–#13 → 3,280

TOTAL INCOME 2,880 / 3,865

PROOF TOTALS:
| – | 36 | 222 | 18 | 63 | 33 | 19 | 49 | 40 | 31 | 1 | 2 | 61 |

ADD BEGINNING CASH, CHECKS AND TOTAL MONTHLY INCOME
ADD ENDING CASH, CHECKING, TOTAL OUTGO →
PROJECTED BUDGET LESS MONTHLY TOTALS

FORM #2

Step 2: Analyze Your Income and Outgo Monthly

Everything you have done up to this point has been gathering facts and organizing them so you can prudently analyze them and establish a lifestyle and budget plan that brings glory to God and meets your needs. Your next step is to analyze each category at the end of every month to determine how your monthly total compares with your projected budget.

If you have overspent in any category, you could then look back over the past month to see day by day if you could have done better. If so, you can double your efforts to improve next month in that category. Your overspending could be because you planned to cut back or do without an item but you kept right on spending and disregarded your plan. If that is your analysis, you need to recommit to follow the plan next month.

If your overspending continues in the same category for three more months and you have done everything possible to follow your cutback plan, then you may have cut back that category's projected budget unrealistically. If that is the case, you may need to increase your budget for that category by decreasing the budget amount in another category.

If you have underspent in any category, you should analyze why. You may have underspent in the auto category for the month because you had no auto repairs and it was not the month to pay for the six-month auto insurance premium. This type of analysis needs no correction or adjustment.

If you undergave to God or undersaved, you should analyze why and correct it by overgiving or oversaving next month. It may take more than one month to correct it.

The importance of keeping good records will be seen as you analyze each category each month. When you keep good, accurate records by recording all income and outgo daily on your Form 2s, it makes your monthly analysis clear and easy.

Step 3: Adjust Your Budget When Circumstances Change

Coming up with the perfect projected budget with your first effort is unlikely. You should do the best you can and then keep accurate records of income and outgo for at least three months before considering any modifications to your budget.

We suggest that you place your Form 2s for the first three months on top of each other by date and adjust the three pages so only the monthly totals and differences at the bottom of the page can be seen (see sample on the next page). All columns should be lined up so you can add the three totals in each column and divide by three to get your average total for each category. Now compare your quarterly average with your projected budget, which is your monthly average for the year. As you make your comparisons, most likely every category will be different. That does not mean that you should modify or change your projected budget at this time. The other three-quarters of the year may not be the same average as the past quarter.

If you are overspending in the food category or any category for all three months, it could be because you are not following your plan to cut back your spending on food, or it could be because you unrealistically underbudgeted your allocation for food.

When you have an unrealistic amount allocated in any category, you need to look at all other categories to see if you can cut back somewhere and increase the unrealistic amount. Your increases need to be offset by decreases totaling the same amount. Only modify those categories that have large differences that cannot wait for your six-month analysis.

We suggest that you analyze the first year of your projected budget quarterly for possible modifications, but make changes only when necessary. If your income changes substantially during the year, either up or down, you may need to modify your budget immediately.

"REAL-LIFE RESULTS FROM CFC COUNSELEES"

ATTITUDE

My husband and I were getting farther and farther behind in our debts. We found after counseling that we had an attitude problem and a definite lack of discipline. Within four months on our new budget we are caught up, and two of our three debts will be paid off within the year. We now give our tithes faithfully with joy, and God is faithful to us for trusting Him.

Summary

In summary, keep daily records of income and outgo. Analyze your income and outgo at the end of each month, and seek ways to improve the next month. Then analyze your income and outgo quarterly for possible changes in your projected budget.

QUARTERLY
BUDGET CONTROL

CURRENT MONTHLY INCOME AND OUTGO RECORD
USE PENCIL — Record every penny daily.

ONE EXAMPLE SHOWING HOW TO ANALYZE EACH CATEGORY
MONTHLY PROJECTED BUDGET FOR FOOD $238

Beginning Cash $3,130
Beginning Checking

Ending Cash $86
Ending Checking $499

DESCRIPTION OF COLUMNS #1–#12	TITHE (GOD)	TAXES (GOV'T)	HOUSING	FOOD GROCERY	AUTO	INSURANCE	DEBTS	ENTER. REC.	CLOTHING	SAVINGS	INVESTMENTS	MEDICAL	MISC. 13	DESCRIPTION OF MISC. ONLY #13
PROJECTED BUDGET →	313	437	770	238	160	313	427	100	32	54	—	35	251	PROJECTED OUTGO
1 Mortgage – Life Ins. – Master Card			731.00			118.00	74.00						4.00	Lunch at School
2 Christian Financial Coun. – Sears		15.00							48.00				7.00	Hair Cut
3 Christian Radio	10.00												12.00	Shower Gift
4 Publix – Gas – Video				58.21	18.00			2.00					.75	Coke
5 Bob 880.00 IRS – SS – Health Ins.	I 55.38 / S 54.56					134.30				12.00			10.00	Beauty Parlor
6 Babysitter – Dr. Tooth	M 12.76							9.00 / 12.71				35.00		
7 Church – Dining Out	72.00													
8 (None)													4.00	Lunch at School
9 Elec – Tel – Water – Visa	E 105.11 / T 62.81						98.00						1.00	Toll – Bridge
10 Master Card – Dr. Jones	W 51.81						74.00					42.00	5.41	Lunch at Work
11 Publix – Gas				56.11	16.82								11.15	Drug Store
12 Sue 560.00 IRS – SS – Med – Ballgame	I 34.12 / S 34.12							7.25		12.00			36.14	K-Mart
13 (None)	M 8.12													
14 Church	72.00													
15 Trash – Publix – Uncle Ben			18.11	11.24			40.00						4.00	Lunch at School
16 JC Penney									24.11				5.00	Dry Cleaner
17 (None)														
18 Publix – Gas				61.71	17.98								4.81	Lunch at Work
19 Bob 880.00 IRS – SS – Med – Health Ins	I 55.81 / S 54.56					134.30				12.00			4.63	Birthday Cards
20 Lawn Care – Grease & Oil	M 12.76				24.11								26.81	Birthday Gift
21 Church – Dining Out	72.00							13.62						
22 ABC Mower – Med. Reimburse							60.00					40.00	4.00	Lunch at School
23 2nd Natl – Savings Withdrawal							41.00			−25.00				
24 Dr. Butcher							10.00						3.86	Ice Cream Cones
25 Publix – Gas				54.21	21.00					12.00			21.11	Drug Store
26 Sue 560.00 IRS – SS – Med – Ballgame	I 34.12 / S 34.12							6.40					4.15	Lunch at Work
27 (None)	M 8.12													
28 Church	72.00													
29 Publix – Visa				14.18			49.00						4.00	Lunch at School
30 (None)													134.00	Child Care
31 (None)														

TOTAL INCOME $2,880

MONTHLY TOTALS →	313	401	992	256	97	280	446	51	72	23	—	37	312	TOTAL OUTGO #1–#13
ADD BEGINNING CASH, CHECKS AND TOTAL MONTHLY TOTALS	—	36	222	18	63	33	19	49	40	31	—	2	61	3,280
PROJECTED BUDGET LESS MONTHLY TOTALS														ADD ENDING CASH, CHECKING, TOTAL OUTGO → 3,865

$3,865

TOTAL INCOME $2,980

MONTHLY TOTALS →	323	401	752	262	109	291	456	63	21	48	—	16	210	TOTAL OUTGO #1–#13
ADD BEGINNING CASH, CHECKS AND TOTAL MONTHLY TOTALS	0	36	18	24	51	22	29	37	11	6	—	19	41	ADD ENDING CASH, CHECKING, TOTAL OUTGO →
PROJECTED BUDGET LESS MONTHLY TOTALS														2,652

TOTAL INCOME $3,180

MONTHLY TOTALS →	328	401	768	266	207	241	430	78	26	48	—	30	242	TOTAL OUTGO #1–#13
ADD BEGINNING CASH, CHECKS AND TOTAL MONTHLY TOTALS	15	36	2	28	47	22	3	22	2	6	—	5	9	ADD ENDING CASH, CHECKING, TOTAL OUTGO →
PROJECTED BUDGET LESS MONTHLY TOTALS														3,115

784 ÷ 3 = $261 QUARTERLY AVERAGE FOR FOOD
261 − 238 = $23 AVERAGE MONTHLY OVERSPENDING FOR FOOD

FORM #2

CHAPTER 10
HOW TO BREAK DOWN YOUR PAYCHECK TO FIT YOUR BUDGET (FORM 1)

The obvious question after you have established a balanced monthly budget is how to break down your "take home" paycheck to meet your monthly budget figures. Some people are paid weekly (52 paydays per year), others are paid biweekly (26 paydays per year), and still others are paid twice monthly (24 paydays per year). The easiest pay method to calculate is for those who are paid monthly (12 paydays per year), and the next easiest are for those who are paid semimonthly (24 paydays per year). Still others are on commission or self-employed with variable income. We will discuss variable incomes later in this chapter.

Take your Form 1 with your Budget Projections completed in the boxes provided, and identify the source of funds and method of payment to be used in paying for each outgo item. Try to be consistent all year long, using the same method of payment.

Step 1: Identify Each Budget Outgo Item to Be Paid by Cash

Identify each budget outgo item to be paid by cash with the letter *C* to the left of each cash item (see sample). Then total all amounts of your projected budget to get the amount of cash you need monthly to pay for all the items you designated to be paid with cash. Now take the monthly total of cash needed, multiply it by 12 to get the cash needed per year, and then divide that amount by the number of paydays you have per year (24, 26, 52). The result is the amount of cash you need from each paycheck.

Step 2: Identify Each Budget Item to Be Saved

Identify the budget items to be saved with the letter *S* to the left of the save item. Then repeat the same process as in Step 1: Multiply the amount to be saved per month times 12, and then divide that amount by the number of paydays per year to determine the amount to be put into savings each payday.

Step 3: Identify Each Budget Item to Be Escrowed

Identify the budget items that are paid less frequently than monthly with an *E* for escrow (reserve) to the left of each escrow item. Items in this category include such things as auto license plate tags, auto insurance, vacations, gifts, medical bills, and real estate taxes. When all escrowed items are identified, repeat the same process as Step 1. Multiply the amount to be escrowed per month times 12 to compute the amount to be escrowed per year. Then divide that amount by the number of paydays per year to determine the amount to be put in an escrow account each payday. Do not place your escrow money in your savings account. We suggest a separate account. If you comingle the two accounts, you will not know how much you have saved for the future and how much you have to pay for those items that are paid less frequently than monthly. You could use an interest-bearing checking account, money market fund, or separate savings account for your escrowed money, as long as you use it for your escrowed items only.

AVERAGE MONTHLY INCOME AND OUTGO FOR THE PAST CALENDAR YEAR

AD = Automatic Deduction
C = CASH   CK = CHECK
E = ESCROW   S = SAVINGS

PAY CHECK BREAKDOWN

PAST   PROJECTED

FROM Jan 1, 08 TO DEC 31, 08

	PAST	PROJECTED
GROSS INCOME PER MONTH	3,000	3,130
Salary, Pension, Soc Sec (His)	1,733	1,907
Salary, Pension, Soc Sec (Hers)	1,040	1,213
Interest and dividends	5	10
Net from Investments/Rents	—	—
Gifts and Inheritance	50	—
Tax Refunds	72	—
Other LOAN	100	—

OUTGO PER MONTH

		PAST	PROJECTED
CK	**1. Tithe and Offering**	90	313
AD	**2. Taxes** (IRS - Soc. Sec.-Med.)	444	437
	NET SPENDABLE INCOME (GROSS INCOME MINUS LINES 1 & 2) ALSO LIST ON LINE A BELOW)	2,466	2,380
	3. Housing	1,068	770
CK	Mortgage (Rent)	621	421
E	House Insurance	32	28
E	Real Estate Taxes	78	80
CK	Electricity / Gas / Oil	107	97
CK	Telephone	62	36
CK	Water & Sewage	54	54
CK	Trash Removal	18	18
CK	Maintenance	41	36
	Cable TV	23	—
	Other FURNITURE	32	—
C	**4. Food (Grocery Store)**	269	238
	5. Auto (Transportation)	487	160
	Payments	288	—
C	Gas	96	84
E	Auto Insurance	48	37
E	License Tag	3	3
CK	Repairs / Maintenance	52	36
	Vehicle Replacement	—	—
	6. Insurance	324	313
E	Life	22	22
AD	Health	291	291
	Other DISABILITY	11	—

		PAST	PROJECTED	
	7. DEBTS	333	427	✸
CK	Credit Cards	268	327	
CK	Installment Loans	40	60	
CK	Other UNCLE BEN	25	40	
	8. Enter/Recreation	173	100	
C	Dining Out	45	20	
E	Trips / Vacation	58	54	
C	Babysitters	18	9	
C	Activities	26	13	
C	Video Rentals	8	4	
	Other BOAT	18	—	
C	**9. Clothing (Cash)**	42	32	
S	**10. Savings (+or-)**	-74	54	✸
	11. Investments (+or-)	—	—	✸
	12. Medical Expenses	87	35	
E	Doctor	56	21	
E	Dentist	12	10	
E	Prescriptions	7	4	
	Other GLASSES	12	—	
	13. Miscellaneous	367	251	
C	Drugstore Items	21	16	
C	Beauty / Barber	22	12	
C	Laundry / Dry Cleaning	5	5	
C	Lunch (Work / School)	64	32	
	Subscriptions	9	—	
E	Gifts (Incl Christmas)	58	30	
	Special Education	—	—	
C	Pocket Money	43	22	
	Pet Store / Veterinarian	11	—	
CK	Other CHILD CARE	134	134	

	PAST	PROJECTED
TOTAL EXPENSES (3-13) (ALSO LIST ON LINE B BELOW)	3,076	2,380
A. NET SPENDABLE INCOME	2,466	2,380
B. LESS EXPENSES (3-13)	3,076	2,380
C. DIFFERENCE/MONTH (+OR-) (LINE A MINUS LINE B)	-610	—
D. DIFFERENCE/YEAR (+OR-) (MULTIPLY LINE C X 12)	-7,320	—

INSTRUCTIONS

Insert only "Past" income and outgo on the lines—after chapter 7 insert only "Projected" income and outgo in the boxes.

Use pencil—use the most accurate figures possible. Fill every blank; if no amount, insert a dash (—).

Round all figures off to the nearest dollar (for example, 941.36 should be 941, and 941.82 should be 942).

Convert all weekly figures to monthly (for example, $100/week x 52 weeks = $5,200/year ÷ 12 months = $433/month).

If self-employed do NOT include business income and use only your net profit from the business that was brought home for the family's use.

✸ Do these 3 projections last and divide your abundance among them only when planning your budget projections.

FORM #1

PAY CHECK BREAKDOWN

(From Form #1)

Bob and Sue are both paid biweekly, they both have 26 pay days per year.

AD - Automatic Deduction

Taxes (IRS-SS-Med) ... 437
Health Insurance 291
$728/mo

C - Cash Needed Per Pay

Food 238
Gas 84
Dining Out 20
Babysitters 9
Activities 13
Video Rentals 4
Clothing 32
Drugstore 16
Beauty/Barber 12
Laundry/Cleaning 5
Lunch .... ·32
Pocket Money 22
$487/mo

S - Savings Deposit Per Pay

Savings   **$54/mo**

CK - Checking Deposit Per Pay

Tithe & Offering 313
Mortgage 421
Electric 97
Telephone 36
Water 54
Trash 18
House Maintenance 36
Auto Repairs 36
Credit Cards 327
Loan 60
Uncle Ben 40
Child Care 134
$1,572/mo

E - Escrow Deposit Per Pay

House Insurance 28
Real Estate Taxes 80
Auto Insurance 37
License Tag 3
Life Insurance 22
Trips/Vacations 54
Doctor 21
Dentist 10
Prescriptions 4
Gifts 30
$289/mo

SUMMARY CALCULATIONS:

Automatic Deductions — No pay check breakdown needed as these items are automatically deducted.

Cash Needed Per Pay —
$487 x 12 months = $5,844 + 26 pay days = $225 per pay

Checking Needed Per Pay —
$1,572 x 12 months = $18,864 + 26 pay days = $725 per pay

Escrow Deposit Per Pay —
$289 x 12 months = $3,468 + 26 pay days = $133 per pay

Savings Deposit Per Pay —
$54 x 12 months = $648 + 26 pay days = $ 25 per pay

CHART 10.1

PAY CHECK BREAKDOWN BETWEEN HUSBAND AND WIFE

Bob's monthly income is $1,907   per month or $ 880   biweekly.
Sue's monthly income is $1,213   per month or $ 560   biweekly.

Combined Total $3,120   per month $1,440   biweekly

Bob's Income is $ 1,907 ÷ $ 3,120 or 61 % of the Total Income.
Sue's Income is $ 1,213 ÷ $ 3,120 or 39 % of the Total Income.

Category	Bob/Pay Day	Sue/Pay Day	Combined Total Per Pay Day
Automatic Deduction	61% x $336 = $205	39% x $336 = $131	$205 + $131 = $336
Cash	61% x $225 = $138	39% x $225 = $ 87	$138 + $ 87 = $225
Checking	61% x $725 = $443	39% x $725 = $282	$443 + $282 = $725
Escrow	61% x $133 = $ 81	39% x $133 = $ 52	$ 81 + $ 52 = $133
Savings	61% x $ 21 = $ 13	39% x $ 21 = $ 8	$ 13 + $ 8 = $ 21
TOTALS	**$880**	**$560**	**$1,440**

NOTE: The difference between $25 on Chart 10.1 and the $21 amount on the above chart in the Savings category is from interest earned on the savings balance, it is not from either pay check.

This example is only one way the breakdown could be divided between the husband and the wife. If you find a different way that works for you, use it!

CHART 10.2

Step 4: Identify Each Budget Item That Is Already Allocated

Identify the budget items that are already allocated by your employer to be withheld from your pay with the letters *AD* for automatic deduction to the left of the automatic deducted items. Items in this category include IRS withholding, Social Security withholding, Medicare withholding, life and health insurance premiums, union dues, and various types of pension plan withholding or savings plans. These are all items that are already allocated for you by your employer. In some mortgage payments, the lender has an escrow account and withholds to pay your real estate taxes and house insurance. If so, you could include those items as *AD*, because you do not need to establish a separate allocation to pay them. The payment for them is included in your mortgage payment.

Step 5: Identify Each Budget Item to Be Paid by Check

Identify the items that you plan to pay by check with a *CK*. When you cash your paycheck, you will now know how to break down your allocation: a certain amount in cash, an amount for checking, an amount for escrow, and an amount for savings.

Those with variable income could establish a "barrel" system, in which all income from every source and any amount is deposited in a so-called barrel account. Then salary yourself from that barrel account, just as if you were employed and receiving a fixed regular income.

Now follow the same steps 1 through 5, as previously described. If your barrel account is not sufficient to support your family budget need, you need to evaluate the situation from two perspectives. First, look for ways to increase the income going into the barrel, ways to reduce the outgo from the barrel, and ways to control future spending from the barrel. This is especially true for self-employed persons. If you are unable to solve your problem from the business or variable income barrel account, then the second perspective is to look for ways to alter your family lifestyle so your existing barrel is sufficient to provide for your family needs. You may also want to apply the principles learned in this book to running your business. Reduced expenses in the business may free up more money for personal income. You should especially consider running all legitimate expenses through your business to obtain tax advantages.

Step 6: Avoid Spending When an Item Is Not Budgeted

When all income is allocated for a designated category, you must avoid spending for items not budgeted, or you will be living beyond your means, unless you modify your budget before buying. If you want to buy a $500 item that is not in your projected budget plan, you can see if there is any $500 allocation in the projected budget that has a lower priority than the $500 item you want to buy. If so, then you could substitute the unbudgeted $500 item for the lower priority projected budget item. This is a way to avoid overspending and borrowing, which is more critical as the months and years go by. We urgently need to get out of debt and stay out of debt.

Another option to avoid overspending is to evaluate if the wanted $500 item has a higher priority than saving for the future. If so, we could withdraw from our existing savings and pay cash for the wanted item.

Summary

Discipline yourself to break down your paycheck into specific amounts of cash or amounts to deposit into various accounts. Stick to your plan and limit your spending to budgeted items. If your plan works on paper, it will work in reality. You should not decide to spend based on the cash in your pocket or the balance in your checkbook. Once you have a balanced budget, you should only spend based on the amount allocated in your projected budget, because all dollars coming in are already allocated to go out. If you do not follow your written plan, you will have wasted the time you took to develop it.

"REAL-LIFE RESULTS FROM CFC COUNSELEES"

FAITHFULNESS

When we came to CFC we had to live in a motel room because we didn't have the money to rent an apartment. Within a few months we were able to pay all our bills on time, put money in savings, and live off my husband's salary alone. Over and over God has demonstrated His faithfulness.

PART 4: GUIDES FOR BETTER MANAGING

CHAPTER 11
RECORD KEEPING

Why Keep Records?

Many people who think they have a budget do not—they are simply record keepers. Excellent record keeping is not a budget, but it is essential in preparing, maintaining, and controlling a budget. Proverbs 27:23 (KJV) tells us, *"Be thou diligent to know the state of thy flocks, and look well to thy herds."* Being diligent means paying attention to detail, knowing where you stand. We may not be shepherds, but the principle taught here is that we need to know what we have and keep abreast of where it is and how it is being managed. Be diligent—keep good records!

Record Keeping for Couples

Both spouses should be aware of all budget matters, but only one at a time should be the record keeper. Why? Because, as the saying goes, "Everybody's job is nobody's job." The wife says, "I thought you were going to pay the bill." The husband says, "I thought you were going to pay the bill." The result: no one paid the bill.

Accountability is the key to good record keeping. If one spouse agrees to be the record keeper, then the other spouse must be the reporter and report all income and outgo. When keeping the records for Form 2, Current Monthly Income and Outgo Record, the most important commitment is to record all income and outgo daily at the end of the day. This means that the reporter must report at the end of the day, to the penny, what came in and what went out for the entire family. This should be done in writing to avoid errors and misunderstandings. If each is accountable for a specific function and each performs that function daily, peace will result, records will be accurate, and God will be pleased. **Having peace in the family about money matters is one of the best insurance policies you can obtain for a long, happy, successful marriage.**

Couples Changing Roles as Record Keeper

God does not say who should be the record keeper, but He tells us to *"develop common sense and good judgment"* (Proverbs 4:7 TLB). It makes good sense for the record keeper to be the one who has the time, does the best job, and enjoys doing it. That does not excuse the other spouse from having any responsibility for or knowledge of finances.

Since no one knows whom God will call home first or when, both husband and wife need to be prepared to be the record keeper without advance notice. We counsel with many widows and widowers who were not the record keeper, and they are lost when it comes to becoming the record keeper overnight. To avoid this from happening in your family, we recommend that the non–record keeper keep all the records for one full year while the record keeper is still here to show the other how to perform this task and to answer questions along the way. Remember, God also expects the survivor to be a wise and faithful manager. One of the greatest acts of love a spouse can perform is to show the non–record keeper how to keep the records before God calls her or him home.

Record Keeper's Responsibilities

The record keeper's responsibilities start with recording all income and outgo daily on Form 2, Current Monthly Income and Outgo Record. Also included is writing all checks, paying all bills, balancing the checkbook monthly, and keeping all records necessary for the budget and income tax purposes. Each person should learn how to prepare income tax returns unless the returns are very complex.

Keep in mind that the non–record keeper should be prepared to do all of the above if and when necessary. Doing so may be necessary during a spouse's long-term illness or for a year or two while the record-keeping spouse is attending school in the evenings. And it may become a full-time responsibility if a spouse is widowed.

On occasions, as a convenience, the non–record keeper may write a check or make several entries in the record keeping. When this is done, the action taken should be discussed with the record keeper as soon as convenient following the action. This will help avoid oversights and duplications. **Under no circumstances should either spouse take action in finances without the other spouse's knowledge**—preferably in advance, but certainly following the action. Again, we apply common sense: a surprise birthday gift can only be entered after the birthday.

How to Balance Your Checkbook

Most of us have not taken a course in school on how to balance a checkbook, and people of all ages have told me they do not know how to do so. Those who balance their checkbooks use slightly different methods. The method is not as important as the result—a balanced checkbook.

The following is one method you could use if you get your checks back with your bank statement:

- Notice that your statement lists your checks in numerical order. If you get your checks back, verify that all the checks are yours and that you or an authorized person signed all the checks.
- Verify that all the deposits you made are listed on your statement.
- Verify that all debits (checks or other withdrawals) and credits on the statement are correct and entered in your check register or on your check stubs.
- Look at your last monthly statement to determine which checks were outstanding and did not clear in time for your last statement.
- Verify that all outstanding checks from last month cleared this month. If not, list them as outstanding again this month.
- Complete the reconciliation form on the back of your bank statement by entering the ending balance of your statement plus any deposits not credited on that statement. From that total, subtract the total of outstanding checks to get your balance. This balance should agree with your checkbook balance after entering in your checkbook all charges, deductions, and interest shown on that statement.

If your account does not balance, check the following:

- Have you entered the amount of each check in your checkbook accurately?
- Are all deposit amounts, including interest, entered in your checkbook as shown on the bank statement?
- Have all charges been deducted from your checkbook?
- Have you double-checked the additions and subtractions in your checkbook?
- Have you brought the correct balance forward from one checkbook page to another?
- Have all checks written and other withdrawals been deducted from your checkbook?

If you have done all the above and it still does not balance, it is time to seek help from a qualified person or from your bank. Yes, it is possible—it could be a bank error.

Summary

Good record keepers are more content and experience a greater peace about money matters, which for married persons results in a happier marriage. Good records are necessary for developing an effective, efficient balanced budget that pleases God and meets your needs.

CHAPTER 12
EARNING

Earn an Honest Living

Does it really make a difference how we get our money? According to the Bible, it does make a difference. Paul exhorts his readers in Ephesians 4:28 (TLB), *"If anyone is stealing he must stop it and begin using those hands of his for honest work."* We feel good about ourselves when we have a good honest job. It gives us high self-esteem, high self-worth, and a sense of accomplishment in being able to provide for our family and ourselves.

As Christians, we are here to serve, not to be served. This Christlike attitude of serving can best be done when we are working in an honest business environment, with honest practices, honest prices, and honest people. God is pleased, and we are blessed when we earn our money honestly and serve others honestly.

It is not how much we earn but how we earn it that is important to God. *"A little, gained honestly, is better than great wealth gotten by dishonest means"* (Proverbs 16:8 TLB). God does not want us to engage in any dishonest methods of receiving money. Dishonesty is not only disobedient to God; it is also against the law.

We can be dishonest in little and big ways. If we arrive to work late, leave early, and overstay breaks or lunch, we are stealing time from our employer, which is dishonest. Overcharging is dishonest; charging different people different amounts for the same product or service is not being fair or honest. The obvious big ways of being dishonest are being involved in unlawful businesses or unlawful practices, including deceptive means to evade paying taxes.

Our purpose in life as Christians is to bring glory to God every day in every way, including the way we earn our income. Is God pleased with the way we are now earning our income? If not, we should seek His wisdom and His direction to change whatever needs to be changed so that we are being obedient to God.

Work Smarter, Not Harder

Many people are working long hours on one, two, or three jobs to earn more money. Some people want more money to have more pleasure or for self-centered reasons. Others are working long hours just to provide for their family's basic needs. Many times we are so busy with the urgent we don't have time for the important.

God wants us to have balance in our lives. We have heard the expression "All work and no play makes Jack a dull boy." Well, God wants us to be the spouse we should be, the parent we should be, and the provider we should be, all in a proper balance. It takes a wise person to organize time to keep all three in balance. And since *"the LORD grants wisdom"* (Proverbs 2:6 TLB), we should pray and seek God's wisdom to plan a balance.

We learn in Psalm 127:2 (TLB) that *"it is senseless for you to work so hard. . .fearing you will starve to death; for God wants his loved ones to get their proper rest."* It appears that God wants us to work smarter not harder. One way to do that is to establish a budget so we can spend more wisely what we make. Another way is to work more effectively and efficiently at what we do by being accurate, better organized, and faster at our job. When we excel at our work, we are worth more to our employer and usually receive more pay, giving us the ability to attain that balance more easily and spend more time with spouse and children.

The Myth of the Working Mother

Some families think the solution to their so-called financial problem is for the wife to go to work. It may be a solution, but not necessarily so. It could even increase the problem.

Take the wife who has not worked before and has no professional training and who would probably receive minimum wage on her first job. She has one preschool child to place in a child-care center, and she needs to drive to work. Her income and expenses may look like Chart 12.1.

As we analyze the example in Chart 12.1, we see she is spending $80 per week to place her child in a day-care center; $39 per week is withheld for her federal income taxes; $23 per week is needed to provide transportation to and from work; $26 per week is her tithe commitment to God; $20 per week is withheld for Social Security and Medicare; $11 per week extra is spent on food that can be prepared more quickly because she doesn't have time to cook from scratch; $8 per week is needed to keep up her work clothes inventory; $6 per week covers pizza or a bucket of chicken when she runs out of quick meals; $6 per week goes for more cosmetics and more frequent hair care; and in the miscellaneous category, $3 per week is put toward snacks and drinks she purchases during breaks and toward various collections taken for showers, birthdays, retirement, and going-away parties and gifts.

When we add up all the expenses that are incurred just because she is working, we see that she is working 40 hours per week and her net spendable income may only be $38 per week, less than $1 per hour, while someone else is raising her child. After gathering and analyzing all the facts, we need to be honest with ourselves and ask if it is worth it.

If this woman had two children in child care, she might just break even with no net spendable income. **This is only a sample of what may happen. Every working mother should place her own figures in this example to determine her net spendable income.**

While many working mothers may be surprised to know what their net spendable income really is, that is not the myth! When the wife goes to work, most couples think they can take that luxury vacation or buy a newer car or eat out more often. The average family may end up spending 80 percent of their gross income, when they only had 20 percent to spend. The result—they are 60 percent worse off than if she had not gone to work.

Please understand that it is not only a matter of whether the wife works. If she does work, how much can she expect to net after her expenses for working are subtracted? The family needs to fix their spending level so the net spendable income can be used for the intended purpose for which she goes to work. Many wives go to work just to pay the bills. Others save for a specific reason, such as the down payment on a house, a second car, the children's college education, or to place the children in a private school.

Many couples come for counseling to establish a budget that will allow them to live on one income so the wife can stay home and raise the children, a God-given responsibility. It is not wrong for mothers to work; every mother should have peace about her decision spiritually, emotionally, and financially. Some mothers have no job skills and would only earn minimum wage, while other mothers may be professionally trained and may earn as much as or more than their husbands. Every mother has a different set of financial facts and vocational skills, so no one answer is right for all mothers.

My intent is to help mothers gather the facts and analyze the options so they can make the right decision based on their circumstances.

THE MYTH OF THE WORKING MOTHER

$260 — GROSS WEEKLY INCOME

ITEMIZED WEEKLY EXPENSES

$80	Child care (1 child)	31%
$39	IRS taxes.	15%
$23	Transportation	9%
$26	God (her tithe).	10%
$20	Social Security/Medicare.	8%
$11	Quick meals at home	4%
$8	Work clothes	3%
$6	Carry-out meals.	2%
$6	Haircuts and cosmetics.	2%
$3	Miscellaneous (drinks, gifts, etc.)	1%

GROSS WEEKLY INCOME	$260	
Minus TOTAL WEEKLY EXPENSES	−$222	**85%**
WEEKLY NET SPENDABLE	$38	**15%**

CHART 12.1

If Self-Employed, Salary Yourself

Many people who have variable income or are self-employed think they cannot establish a budget because they never know when they will have income or how much they will bring in. The good news is that God wants to give us wisdom, common sense, and good judgment. So let's take a common-sense approach to converting variable income into a steady, fixed income.

Step 1: Select a business checking account for your business. All income from your business goes into the business account, and all business expenses, which must be kept separate from family expenses, should be paid out of your business account before you pay yourself.

Step 2: Set a fixed salary for yourself to be paid weekly, biweekly, or on a set plan of your choosing. When you do this, you will enjoy peace about regular steady income. The salary should be based on your family budget need, which this book helps you to establish.

Step 3: If your business account overflows with an abundance, what do you do? One option is to honor the Lord from your abundance. Another option is to give yourself a bonus as often as necessary from your business account. We strongly suggest that you predetermine what you are going to do with your abundance if and when you have a surplus. That decision may help you make a wise decision, such as getting out of debt or saving for a specific purpose. It could help to keep you from spending it foolishly or impulsively.

Step 4: If your business account is empty and you can't pay your salary, what do you do? Analyze your business! What can you do to increase the income? What can you do to reduce the business expenses? And what can you do to control future spending? If you have done everything possible to increase income, reduce outgo, and control future spending, and you can't do anything more, then analyze your family budget for ways to alter your lifestyle and your budget so your business can support your family. You may need to consider changing your business or going to work for someone on a salary basis if your business cannot provide for your family.

Keep Personal and Business Records Separate

One of the biggest problems among self-employed persons (part-time or full-time) in small businesses is that they do not keep good records that report all business matters separate from personal matters. The result of mixing business and personal funds and records is confusion. We don't even know our true profit.

Use one checking account for business and another checking account for personal expenses. When an expense is both personal and business—for example, you use a business vehicle for personal use or vice versa—what do you do? If you determine from an accurate mileage record that 80 percent of the total mileage on a vehicle is for business, pay all of that vehicle's expenses from your business account. Then pay your business 20 percent of the total vehicle expenses from your personal checking account. This would be like leasing your business vehicle 20 percent of the time for personal use. Keeping separate and accurate records will allow you to know your true profit. No matter what method you use, keep business and personal records separate!

CHAPTER 13
GIVING

Stewardship may be considered to be three phases:

1. Earning money
2. Possessing money
3. Giving money

Our purpose as Christians is found in 1 Corinthians 10:31: *"Whatsoever ye do, do all to the glory of God"* (KJV). As Christians we should bring glory to God in every area of our lives, including the way we earn money, manage money, and give away money.

The way to honor God is to be obedient to God's Word and God's ways. What are God's ways of managing money? He first tells us to work hard and earn it honestly. Then He tells us to honor Him with the first part (10 percent). And finally, He tells us to save for the future, provide for our families, and give to the needy.

Our stewardship includes giving of our time, talent, and treasure. Most people find the easiest of these three to be our treasure. However, today, due to the economic problems we as a nation are experiencing, many people are not honoring God first in the giving of the tithe, and they are missing out on God's blessing that He promised us in Malachi 3:10. God said we are robbing Him if we are not tithing—giving God the first part (10 percent) of our income on a regular basis. The tithe should go to your church; then you can give to other ministries and to needy people.

God also tells us to give cheerfully: *"Every man according as he purposeth in his heart, so let him give; not grudgingly, or of necessity: for God loveth a cheerful giver"* (2 Corinthians 9:7 KJV). Moreover, we read that *"it is more blessed to give than to receive"* (Acts 20:35 KJV). To give any amount for any reason, we need to follow God's way to manage money; then we experience the greater blessing. But we are also told to give what we have, not what we don't have: *"If you are really eager to give, then it isn't important how much you have to give. God wants you to give what you have, not what you haven't. Of course, I don't mean that those who receive your gifts should have an easy time of it at your expense"* (2 Corinthians 8:12–13 TLB).

CHAPTER 14
SAVING

Since God owns everything—including all of our possessions—we have a responsibility and accountability to Him for the way we manage money while we pass through life. While God owns it all, He wants us to enjoy it. We find His ownership and His plan for us to enjoy it in 1 Corinthians 10:26 (TLB): *"For the earth and every good thing in it belongs to the Lord and is yours to enjoy"*

If we are not enjoying what God has provided, it is not His fault. We need to look in the mirror and ask God, "What do You want me to change so that I can enjoy what You have provided?" Something—our attitude, our priorities, or our actions—needs to change if we are not enjoying what God has provided.

One of the most important priorities of money—after earning it honestly and honoring God with the first part—is to SAVE FOR THE FUTURE. *"The wise man saves for the future, but the foolish man spends whatever he gets"* (Proverbs 21:20 TLB). The average U.S. family is living on credit and is NOT wise (saving for the future) and NOT foolish (spending whatever they get), but is MORE THAN FOOLISH (spending more than they receive).

Proverbs 21:5 (TLB) teaches us, *"Steady plodding brings prosperity; hasty speculation brings poverty."* Starting early in life to save little by little on a regular basis will lead you to financial prosperity. A good commonsense reason to save for the future is that we don't know what the future may bring.

In saving for the future, we should avoid get-rich-quick schemes, as Proverbs 28:22 (TLB) warns: *"Trying to get rich quick is evil and leads to poverty."*

SAVINGS GOAL	
1st level	3 months' gross salary
2nd level	6 months' gross salary
3rd level	9 months' gross salary
4th level	12 months' gross salary
Keep in liquid assets.	

CHART 14.1

Chart 14.1 is a suggested guide for the future. *"The wise man saves for the future."* It may take several years to reach the fourth level, but do NOT give up.

SAVINGS GROWTH

Select the amount per month you want to save, then save that amount every month.
(All figures are based on 5 percent compounded daily)

SAVING FOR THE FUTURE

IF YOU SAVE:	FOR:	YOU WILL ACCUMULATE	YOU CAN WITHDRAW FOREVER
$ 20.00 / month	10 years	$ 3,120.00	$ 13.00 / month
	15 years	$ 5,373.00	$ 22.00 / month
	20 years	$ 8,265.00	$ 34.00 / month
	30 years	$ 16,746.00	$ 70.00 / month
	40 years	$ 30,729.00	$ 128.00 / month
$ 20.00/month is 5% of $400.00/month or $ 4,800/year			
$ 50.00 / month	10 years	$ 7,801.00	$ 32.00 / month
	15 years	$ 13,432.00	$ 56.00 / month
	20 years	$ 20,662.00	$ 86.00 / month
	30 years	$ 41,865.00	$ 174.00 / month
	40 years	$ 76, 821.00	$ 319.00 / month
$ 50.00/month is 5% of $1,000.00/month or $ 12,000.00/year			
$ 100.00 / month	10 years	$ 15,601.00	$ 65.00 / month
	15 years	$ 26,863.00	$ 112.00 / month
	20 years	$ 41,323.00	$ 172.00 / month
	30 years	$ 83,729.00	$ 348.00 / month
	40 years	$ 153,643.00	$ 639.00 / month
$ 100.00/month is 5% of $ 2,000.00/month or $24,000.00/year			

CHART 14.2

Chart 14.2 shows how systematic saving started early can assure you a greater steady income for the rest of your life as you get older and may not be physically able to work.

CHAPTER 15
BUYING

Determine the Real Need

Too little income is not the problem; overspending for one's income level is where most people find themselves. One way to correct this matter is to determine our real need before we spend. Our basic needs are food, shelter, and clothing. Above those essentials, we need to honor God, pay our taxes, and secure transportation so that we can provide income. A budget helps us get all these needs organized. Good health and a good mind enable us to earn the money to meet the needs.

After honoring the Lord and paying our taxes, we now have what we call discretionary spending to provide necessary items—food, shelter, clothing, and transportation. We need to analyze and prioritize our needs, wants, and desires. *Needs* are food, shelter, clothing, and, for some people, transportation. *Wants* are food, shelter, clothing, and transportation of a greater quantity or a better quality. We may want more or better clothes, more or better quality food, or a better quality house or car. *Desires* are conveniences, luxuries, and extravagances—things that most of our grandparents got along without and we could get along without.

Now, there is nothing wrong with having our wants and desires if our budget permits it and God gives us a peace about having them. Our needs, wants, and desires are simply a priority list. Our first priority is to provide for the basic needs of our family. When those needs are met, we can move up to our wants—more and better quality. Then when we are able, we can move up to our desires. This priority list should keep us from buying a luxury car or boat when we can't afford to put food on the table.

The bottom line is to be honest with yourself, establish your priorities, and buy your needs first, then wants, and only as you are able, your desires. Seek God's wisdom and direction for your decisions and your peace.

Prepare Need List at Home

To avoid overspending and impulse spending, prepare a list at home of things you need, after looking in your pantry, closet, and garage. If you don't need it after looking in these areas, you don't need it just because it has a sale tag on it in the store.

Starting a list at the beginning of each week and adding to it during the week may be helpful, but only go shopping once a week. If we shop by list only and limit our number of trips to the store, we will experience greater economy and spend less.

Use of Coupons

Many people clip coupons in an effort to save money. To really save money, you should use coupons only (1) if the item is already on your need list and (2) only after you have shopped for price. Do not make up your list from your coupons, or you will buy more than you need. Only use coupons after you made your need list from looking in the pantry, closet, and garage.

When shopping for price, compare various brands for the best price. Also compare various sizes for the best price per ounce. Usually, but not always, the largest size is the best price per ounce. Another comparison is the number of servings per price. You could compare canned vegetables with frozen and fresh, for example, and determine the number of servings you can get from each.

When comparing five-pound bags of rice, one popular brand was priced at $3.39 and offered a $.50 discount coupon. But the store brand was $1.79. The only difference was the price. The popular brand, even with the coupon, was $1.10 more than the store brand. We could throw away the popular brand coupon and save money. It is doubtful that the family at home that ate the rice could identify any difference.

Compare Price, Quality, and Service

Buying the lowest-priced item every time, especially household items and appliances, is not necessarily the wisest choice. We can buy a specific brand item from the store with the lowest price when the quality and service for the identical item are the same as another store. When comparing different brand items, we need to determine how long it will last as well as the price based on the quality of the item. When we buy an item that needs to be serviced, we need to look at the probability of the store being in business when we need service and their reputation for reliable service and reasonable prices. Always look for a balance between price, quality, and service.

Use Cash and Avoid Buying on Credit

According to various surveys, you can save from 28 to 34 percent when you avoid credit and pay cash. Looking at it another way, you will spend 28 to 34 percent more if you buy with credit cards. Merchants will pay credit card companies 3 percent to 5 percent to permit you to use credit cards in their store because they know you are likely to spend more when you use credit. The credit card companies take approximately 5 percent as a loss in their collections, but on an average 18 percent interest charge, they still net 13 percent plus merchant fees.

If you save $28 on every $100 you spend, you will have more money to save, spend, or honor the Lord. This is just another way to find an abundance in your budget. Keep in mind that every dollar you pay in interest is money you are throwing out the window.

Seek Counsel on Big-Ticket Items

None of us knows all that needs to be known about every item we buy, especially big-ticket items. Recall the proverbs we cited earlier: *"What a shame—yes, how stupid!—to decide before knowing the facts!"* (18:13 TLB) and *"Without consultation, plans are frustrated, but with many counselors they succeed"* (15:22 NASB). God wants us to get the facts by seeking counsel from more than one counselor, especially if it is the salesperson.

We have several ways to get the facts and seek counsel. Information on many items can be found in *Consumer Reports Buying Guide*, which is available at most public libraries. We can talk to more than one company representative or salesperson. Another way to get information is to talk to other people who previously bought the item.

Control Impulse Buying

Impulse buying is one of the biggest wastes in our budget. We go to the store to buy two things and come home with ten. We just bought eight items on impulse. Some people say, "I just went to the store to browse," and they came home with three bags full of "browse." We all are guilty of impulse spending to some degree. How do we control impulse spending?

- Carry no credit cards.
- Carry no checks.
- Carry no extra cash.
- Carry only the cash needed to buy those items on your need list, which you prepared at home after looking in the pantry, closet, and garage.

These guidelines may seem rather severe, but they work. When we have no way to impulse spend, we won't spend impulsively. Most people want emergency money in their wallet or pocketbook. I agree that is wise. But I suggest that you select one bill—a $20, $50, or $100—as your emergency money and then place that bill in a hidden location in your wallet so you won't be tempted to spend it. Remember, that bill is emergency money only, and you don't have an emergency every day! That is, you don't spend it every day and then replace it with another bill when you get home. This system will work if you follow the plan.

How to Have Transportation without Monthly Payments

Many people today think that having a monthly payment on a car, truck, or van is a way of life. It is an expensive way to provide transportation. People who trade cars frequently, finance the new car before the old one is paid in full, and put very little down when they trade are in a situation we call upside-down financing. This usually means that at no time during the life of the loan can you sell your car for enough money to pay off the loan. The depreciation on your car makes the value of your car go down faster than the balance of the loan.

Overspending and overborrowing on vehicles is one of the four biggest problem areas in most peoples' budgets. How do we solve this problem?

We can start by only buying a vehicle we can pay for in cash. This may mean beginning with an older car and saving extra money to upgrade with a newer car as we are able. With this plan we could end up buying a new car with all cash in a few years if we establish a budget and follow our plan to save on a regular systematic basis.

Finance Plan

Twenty-six years ago I made a decision about buying a car with limited cash. Chart 15.1 is the information I gathered to make my decision. While the prices are not current, the principle is the same today. The first step is to get the facts, then write them down and analyze them to find the best decision. I obtained the facts about buying a new car (1981) at the end of the year after the next year's (1982) models had come out. The car I looked at was considered one year old but was new because it had no mileage. The sales price was $9,000. If I paid $1,000 down and financed $8,000 for three years at 12 percent interest, the payment would have been $302 per month. The interest would have totaled $2,880, which means I would have paid $11,880 for that $9,000 car. If I wanted lower monthly payments, I could have obtained an $8,000 loan at 12 percent for four years with payments of $247 per month. The interest would have totaled $3,840, which means I would have paid $12,840 to acquire that $9,000 car.

Most people do not realize that the longer the loan, the more interest you pay, and the more you pay to acquire the auto. They are only interested in the lower monthly payment. Many autos today are financed over five, six, and seven years just to keep the monthly payments down so buyers can qualify to finance them. That does not mean they can afford the car or that it is good for their budget.

Cash Plan

Back to my facts. What would happen if I took the $1,000 down payment and bought the best car I could find for $1,000 cash? At that time I could have bought an eight-year-old car for $1,000 cash. Had I done that and then added $3 to the $247, four-year finance plan to total $250 and then started saving $250 per month for 12 months, I would have saved $3,000 cash in one year. Then if I chose to upgrade my transportation by trading or selling my eight-year-old car that would be nine years old, I probably could have gotten $500 for it, which means I would have had $3,500 cash in one year to pay for a newer car. And I probably could have bought a four-year-old car for $3,500.

If I continued to save $250 per month for the second year, I would have had another $3,000. If I decided to upgrade my car at the end of the second year, I probably could have gotten $2,500 for the $3,500 car I bought a year earlier. I would then have had $3,000 plus $2,500, or $5,500, to pay cash for possibly a three-year-old car.

Since the feeling of driving a car without monthly payments is great, I would have continued saving $250 per month for the third year and had another $3,000. If I decided to upgrade again at the end of the third year, I probably could have gotten $4,000 for the $5,500 car I bought one year earlier. I would now have $7,000 cash to buy possibly a two-year-old car. Now, when I compare this point of my cash plan with the purchase of the $9,000 new car on a three-year finance plan, I discover an interesting fact. After three years at $302 a month, that $9,000 car would finally be paid in full, but what would be its value? It would be $4,230—about half the new-car price. I could buy a car for half price if I had patience to wait and saved the cash in advance. Now compare that new car value three years later at $4,230 with the car I could have bought in three years on the cash plan for $7,000. On the finance plan, I could have had a $4,230 car in three years; on the cash plan, I could have had a $7,000 car in three years.

If I projected my cash plan to save $250 per month for the fourth year, I would have saved another $3,000. If I decided to upgrade again at the end of the fourth year, I probably could have gotten $5,000 for the car I bought a year earlier for $7,000, which means I could have had $8,000 to buy a one-year-old car for cash. Now let's compare that $9,000 car financed over four years at $247 per month with the cash plan. That $9,000 car would have been worth $3,150 in four years after it was finally paid for. After four years on the finance plan, I would have had a $3,150 car, but on the cash plan I would have an $8,000 car fully paid. Which is the better plan?

While I do not recommend buying a car every year, we can see that the worst cash plan is better than the best financing plan. If I kept that eight-year-old $1,000 car for four years and saved $250 per month for four years, I would have had $12,000, not including interest.

Many people will ask if it is wise to buy older cars considering the cost of repairs. Let's analyze and see. If I buy a car on a finance plan, I am throwing interest money out the window. If I save on the cash plan, I have money coming in the window. When I add the finance interest I didn't have to pay to the savings interest, that total will go a long way toward paying for repairs on older cars. If I paid $3,840 in interest over four years and I earned 5 percent on my savings for four years (which would be $276), my total saved would be $4,116 available for repairs before it cost me anything.

BUYING A CAR? IT'S YOUR DECISION!

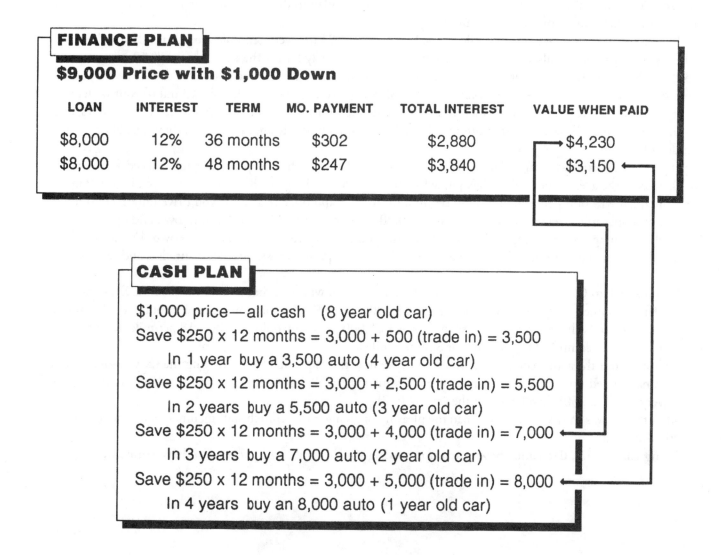

FINANCE PLAN

$9,000 Price with $1,000 Down

LOAN	INTEREST	TERM	MO. PAYMENT	TOTAL INTEREST	VALUE WHEN PAID
$8,000	12%	36 months	$302	$2,880	→ $4,230
$8,000	12%	48 months	$247	$3,840	$3,150 ←

CASH PLAN

$1,000 price—all cash   (8 year old car)
Save $250 x 12 months = 3,000 + 500 (trade in) = 3,500
    In 1 year buy a 3,500 auto (4 year old car)
Save $250 x 12 months = 3,000 + 2,500 (trade in) = 5,500
    In 2 years buy a 5,500 auto (3 year old car)
Save $250 x 12 months = 3,000 + 4,000 (trade in) = 7,000 ←
    In 3 years buy a 7,000 auto (2 year old car)
Save $250 x 12 months = 3,000 + 5,000 (trade in) = 8,000 ←
    In 4 years buy an 8,000 auto (1 year old car)

CHART 15.1

Why don't more people use the cash plan? We don't have money problems; we have ignorance problems and attitude problems about money and money matters. Ignorance—we have not been taught that the cash plan could be so much better. Attitude—we are too proud to drive the oldest car in the parking lot at work, and moreover, we lack discipline. We are not willing to discipline ourselves to save the $250 per month and not spend it for anything else. The cash plan works if we are willing to follow the plan. See chart 15.1 for a better analysis of the finance and cash plans.

Cost per Mile

The bottom line is this: How much does it cost you to drive from point A to point B? The cost per mile will tell you how much (see Chart 15.2).

Column A shows the cost per mile for the $9,000 car financed over a four-year period on the previously stated terms. Column B shows the cost per mile for the same car if purchased for cash. Column C shows the five-year projection for the six-year-old car I bought for $2,000 cash. Column D shows my actual costs and cost per mile for the seven years I had the car.

The way to determine the cost per mile is to add the sales price to the interest and divide that total by the projected number of years you plan to drive a particular car. Your answer will be the average cost per year. Then add the average projected cost per year for insurance, tags, gasoline, and repairs to the average cost per year to acquire the car and divide that total by the estimated miles per year you plan to drive. The answer will be the average cost per mile over the number of years you plan to drive it.

In column A, the average cost per mile was $.30 per mile or $3 for every ten miles you drove. If you drive five miles to buy a gallon of milk and five miles back home, and you pay $4 for the milk, that milk just cost you $7 ($3 + $4). If you really want the impact of what it costs to drive a car, calculate the cost per mile for the car you are driving by using the procedures shown on Chart 15.2. If you arrive at $.30 per mile, take $3 out of your wallet and put it in the auto glove compartment when you drive the first ten miles, then another $3 for the next ten miles, and so on. Most people will say, "I can't afford that." That's right, many people are driving cars they can't afford. They just don't know it.

If you buy an expensive car and drive it few miles and trade often, the cost per mile could exceed $1 per mile, which exceeds the average person's budget guide for an auto. One dollar per mile times an average of 15,000 miles per year equals $15,000 per year, or $1,250 per month, to own and operate a car. If you drive only 10,000 miles per year at $1 per mile average, it would cost you $10,000 per year, or $833 per month, to own and operate a car. I strongly encourage you to compute how much it costs you per mile to drive each car you own. Do not take the estimated costs used by auto rental companies or the IRS, as each person's cost, interest, insurance, and repairs may differ.

Let's go back to Chart 15.2 for a concluding observation. You will note that in column C of the five-year projected plan, I planned to spend $1,000 per year, or $5,000, on a $2,000 car. Some people would say that was a stupid thing to do. Well, the cost per thousand if I spent $1,000 per year would only be $.18 per mile, for a $1,800 per year savings, as compared to column A at $.30 per mile.

Let's work out the actual comparison on paper to see how this is possible. After driving the six-year-old car for seven years, I ended up with a cost per mile of $.15, which was a $2,250 savings per year over column A. I saved more every year ($2,250) than I paid for the car ($2,000).

After the car was thirteen years old, I had the pleasure of giving it to a church staff member who four years later was still driving it!

Using Chart 15.2, determine how much it is costing you per mile and per year to drive your car.

COST PER MILE

	A. FINANCE PLAN	B. CASH PLAN	C. PROJECTED CASH PLANS	D. ACTUAL CASH PLAN
Auto Age	1 YEAR	1 YEAR	6 YEAR	6 YEAR
Sale Price	9,000	9,000	2,000	2,000
Total Interest	3,840	CASH	CASH	CASH
Total Auto Cost	12,840 ÷ 5 Year =	9,000 ÷ 5 Years =	2,000 ÷ 5 Years =	2,000 ÷ 7 Years =
Cost / Year	2,568	1,800	400	285
Insurance / Year	240	240	160	162
Tags / Year	35	35	35	35
Gasoline / Year	1,200	1,200	1,200	1,253
Repairs / Year	500	500	1,000	585
Total Cost / Year	4,543 ÷ 15,000 miles	3,775 ÷ 15,000 miles	2,795 ÷ 15,000 miles	2,320 ÷ 15,000 miles
Cost Per Mile	30¢ / mile	25¢ / mile	18¢ / mile	15¢ / mile
	3.00 / 10 miles	2.50 / 10 miles	1.80 / 10 miles	1.50 / 10 miles
	30.00 / 100 miles	25.00 / 100 miles	18.00 / 100 miles	15.00 / 100 miles
	300.00 / 1000 miles	250.00 / 1000 miles	180.00 / 1000 miles	150.00 / 1000 miles

NOTE: Column D was a savings of $2,250 **each year** over Column A. . . .
More was saved every year over the $2,000 cost of the car.

CHART 15.2

CHAPTER 16
BORROWING

My counsel on the subject of borrowing is **DO NOT BORROW! The overall purpose of this book is to encourage readers to get out of debt and to stay out of debt. It is possible!** At our financial counseling service, we have hundreds of counselees who are debt free and thousands more who are working on plans to become debt free. The process always starts with a budget (a written plan) to increase income, reduce outgo, and control future spending so the counselee can have an abundance to prepay debts and save for future purchases on a cash basis.

Realistically, however, we know that some people are not going to follow our counsel. So before doing any borrowing, the borrower must gather all the facts—how much to borrow, the length of the loan, the interest rate, and the method of computing the interest. Also, one should know the amount of any late charges and penalties. If a borrower plans to prepay, he or she should know the method of computing the payoff or prepayment. Too many people enter into loan contracts without knowing and understanding the facts.

Credit Cards

Credit cards have been the means of overspending for many people, especially for persons with little discipline in controlling their spending. You can use credit cards two ways: as a convenience or as a necessity. If you pay your credit card bills in full every month, you are using them as a convenience. If you are unable to pay all credit cards in full every month, you are using them as a necessity. That is, you don't have the money at home or in the bank or in your pocket, and you can't make a purchase unless you use your credit card. **We encourage every person who chooses to use credit cards to pay them in full every month and to use them only as a convenience.**

When you pay your credit cards in full every month, you avoid the interest, which is usually very high in comparison to other types of loans. Using credit cards is convenient, but no one needs to use them. One can cash checks, buy merchandise, and even rent cars without credit cards. (Yes, I've done it several times in the past.)

A credit card is an easy way to buy now, pay later, but it is a form of borrowing money, and in many cases, a finance charge will be added to your bill each month on the balance you still owe. How much you pay for the use of credit cards depends on three terms of the credit card contract. Creditors must tell you (1) the annual percentage rate (APR), (2) the method of calculating the finance charge, and (3) when the finance charge begins.

On any loan, the interest or finance charge depends on the amount you owe, the interest rate, the length of the loan, and the method of calculating the interest or finance charge. To understand the importance of the method of calculating the interest, see Chart 16.1.

THREE METHODS OF CALCULATING THE FINANCE CHARGE

Method Used	Adjusted Balance	Previous Balance	Average Daily Balance
Monthly Rate	1½%	1½%	1½%
APR-Annual Percentage Rate	18%	18%	18%
Previous Balance	$400	$400	$400
Payments Made in billing period	$300	$300	$300 (on 15th day)
Finance Charge	$1.50	$6.00	$3.75
Rate Times Balance to determine finance charge	1½% x $100	1½% x $400	1½% x $250

The interest is the same on all 3 methods.
The starting balance is the same on all 3 methods.
The payment made is the same on all 3 methods.
Why is the finance charge different?
The method of determining the balance is different in each one so the finance charge is different because the finance charge is determined by multiplying the interest rate times the balance, and the balance in each method is calculated in a different way.

CHART 16.1

In Chart 16.1, with the Adjusted Balance Method, the finance charge is computed after subtracting your payments made during the thirty-day billing period. The Previous Balance Method uses the balance on the first day of the thirty-day billing period and gives you no credit for any payments made in that billing period. In the Average Daily Balance Method, creditors add your balance for each day in the billing period and then divide by the number of days in the billing period to determine the average balance in that period. Most credit cards use the Average Daily Balance Method.

Many creditors in the past did not start a finance charge until the first day of the next billing period, which gave you an "interest free float." You need to read your renewal contracts carefully, as many creditors are now starting to compute interest as of the date of purchase and may back out the interest only if the bill is paid in full by the due date, usually ten to fifteen days. Another caution is to avoid those credit cards that offer lower interest rates but tie their variable rate to the prime rate. If the prime rate goes up, so does your credit card rate. Also, read the fine print on credit card offers of a low or no rate for a period of time to get your business, as most of them will jump your interest rate if you are late or pay less than the minimum amount. Some of the higher rates may be as high as 29 percent.

Auto Loans

Our first encouragement is to buy cars only that you can pay for in cash without financing. If you decide to finance a car, get all the facts about the contract before buying. Pay as much down as possible and borrow for the shortest period of time that your budget will permit. Obtain both the interest rate and the method of computing it. Simple interest on the unpaid balance is the best method for the borrower. You pay interest only on the amount of money you owe each month. This is the same method used for most home mortgages. Another method is the "add-on" method, where interest is computed on the full amount of the loan for the full period of the loan and the total of the principle and interest is divided by the number of payments scheduled to repay the debt. In this method, you are paying interest on money that has already been repaid.

Another fact you need to obtain before borrowing for an auto loan is the method used to determine the payoff, should you decide to prepay the loan from your surplus or from the sale of the car. On "simple interest" loans, the balance and the payoff figures would be the same, with only the daily interest to the exact date of payoff being added. This should be less than thirty days' interest. With "add-on" interest loans, various methods may be used, with one of the more popular methods being the "rule of 78s." This is a short-rate rebate method that gives you back only a portion of your prefigured and precharged interest. With the add-on interest type loan and the rule of 78s pay-off method, even if you pay off the loan in half the time, you do not get half of the interest back.

Please look at Chart 15.1 to compare financing versus the cash plan before buying. Remember, every dollar you pay in interest is money thrown away.

Housing Debt

In 1928, 98 percent of the people who bought a home paid cash; only 2 percent financed their homes. In only forty years, by 1968, only 2 percent of the people who bought a home paid cash, and 98 percent financed their homes. Only a few families today would be able to pay cash for a home. We encourage you to pay all cash if you can. If you can't, put down the most you can and finance the balance over the shortest period of time your budget permits. Then try to prepay your mortgage to get out of debt faster. Your ultimate goal should be to be debt free as soon as possible.

When you shop for a mortgage on your home, get all the facts: the amount you will need as a down payment, the amount you will need to borrow, the total amount of closing costs and fees, the interest rate, the method of computing the interest, the length of the loan, and the amount of monthly payments. Also, does the lender have a prepayment penalty or prepayment privilege? Get the estimated closing date and the amount you need to take to closing, also the type of payment required at closing (usually a cashier's check).

There are a variety of mortgage loans to choose from: conventional, FHA, VA, reverse, and negative amortization. Avoid a negative amortized loan. FHA and VA loans are usually designed for sales with low down payments, and we encourage large down payments when you buy a home.

With FHA loans and other high percentage loans to value, an extra insurance fee is usually charged to help cover the lender's higher risk. You can avoid this additional cost by making a larger down payment. We encourage you to avoid "interest only" loans, because you will be unable to get out of debt or ever have your house paid off. God told us two thousand years ago to "owe no man anything."

A reverse mortgage is designed for those over age sixty-two who have equity in their home, who want to stay in their home but need greater income. If their home has a small mortgage or no mortgage, the reverse mortgage pays off any existing mortgage and starts making a monthly payment to them. That eliminates them making a mortgage payment, and the monthly payments they receive are not taxable income by the IRS.

Chart 16.2 will show you some comparisons with rate and time of repayment.

MORTGAGE COMPARISONS

AMOUNT BORROWED	INTEREST RATE	10 YR LOAN	20 YR LOAN	30 YR LOAN
$20,000		$243/mo.	$159/mo.	$147/mo.
Amount Repaid		$29,160	$38,160	$52,920
Principle Paid	8%	$20,000	$20,000	$20,000
Interest Paid		$9,160	$18,160	$32,920
$20,000		$360/mo.	$308/mo.	$301/mo.
Amount Repaid		$43,200	$73,920	$108,360
Principle Paid	18%	$20,000	$20,000	$20,000
Interest Paid		$23,200	$53,920	$88,360

**Method of Computing Interest —
Simple Interest on the Unpaid Balance–Fixed Rate**

CHART 16.2

Interest Rate Comparison

On Chart 16.2 you will note that on a thirty-year, 8 percent loan, you repay $52,920 for a $20,000 loan, of which $32,920 is for the interest. By comparison, when the interest rate goes up to 18 percent as it did in the early 1980s on the same $20,000 for a thirty-year loan, you will repay $108,360, of which $88,360 is for the interest. Just because of the higher interest rate, you pay $88,360 more for the house over a thirty-year period. Now you can see why you cannot afford to pay higher interest rates.

Time Comparison

On Chart 16.2 you can also note the importance of the length of time over which you repay the loan. The longer the time, the more the cost. The monthly payments on a $20,000 thirty-year, 18 percent loan are $301, compared with $308 for a twenty-year, 18 percent loan. That is only a $7 per month difference between a twenty- and thirty-year loan. For that extra ten years, you pay $34,440 more for your home. The bottom line is that you pay $34,440 less for your home with a twenty-year loan instead of a thirty-year loan, and it takes only $7 per month to do it.

Now, if you like the way that shorter-term loan works with the twenty-year loan, try the ten-year comparison. You pay only $59 per month more for the ten-year, 18 percent, $20,000 loan than for the thirty-year loan, but you save $65,160 in interest, which means you save $65,160 on the total cost of your home.

When you prepay any amount at any time on your existing mortgage, it will shorten the time it takes to pay off the loan, and it will save you an amazing amount of interest. You don't have to take thirty years to pay off a thirty-year loan. By prepaying you could shorten a thirty-year loan to eight, ten, twelve, or fifteen years, depending on the amount and the frequency of prepayments. We suggest that you discuss your prepayment plans with your lender to be sure that the prepayment amounts will be applied directly to the principle and thereby reduce the next month's interest. Prepayments can be made monthly, quarterly, yearly, or any way you desire. The larger the amount and the more frequently they are made, the more you save in interest.

Personal Loans

Personal loans can be obtained from a variety of sources with differing terms. Most personal loans fall into the unsecured type—that is, without any collateral pledged. Some secured loans are also in the personal loan category. The same caution is given as with all other loans. Get the facts, evaluate the options, and do not rush into borrowing until you have time to pray about it and receive peace about it from God.

Personal loans from small loan companies usually carry a higher interest rate than most credit cards. Bank interest rates on personal loans can be slightly lower than most credit cards. Credit unions usually charge less than banks. Personal loans on your whole life insurance policy will often have the lowest interest rate. Interest rates change from time to time and from location to location, so the best way to know which is best for you is to get the facts from all sources before making any decisions.

Nowhere in the Bible does it say to go to the bank or to the government when you need help. Instead, we read in 1 Timothy 5:8 (TLB), *"Anyone who won't care for his own relatives when they need help, especially those living in his own family, has no right to say he is a Christian."* God is telling us that family should help family. Thus, we should help our own relatives when they need help. We need to manage well so that we have an abundance and can help our family from our abundance. Do you have a relative in need?

Let us assume you have a relative paying 18 percent average interest on credit cards and you are receiving 4 percent interest on your savings. If their debts total $10,000 at 18 percent and you have a surplus of $10,000 and you agree to lend them $10,000 at 6 percent interest, guess what just happened? You helped them save 12 percent, and they helped you earn 2 percent more. In this type of personal loan, both gain and no one loses (except for the credit card company). When both needs are met, God receives glory. The terms for every loan to a relative should be made in writing and repaid as agreed.

When making a loan to a relative, you need to use the same wisdom and judgment as if you were lending someone else's money, because you are—you are lending what belongs to God, because He owns it all. If you lend to those who mismanage money, they will continue to mismanage money unless they receive wisdom from God and change their attitudes about spending, borrowing, and living within their income.

We encourage you to look for evidence of responsibility before you lend to a relative. A Chinese proverb says,

"You can give a boy a fish and tomorrow he is hungry, but if you teach him how to fish, he can have food for life." What is more valuable to the boy? Obviously, it is more valuable to know how to fish. The same is true with money. It is more valuable to know how to manage money than to receive money every day. Be sure you offer the wisdom to know how to manage money before you lend to a relative. This book given as a gift is a great place to start in helping them.

If you are the one in need, follow all the steps in this book and do everything you can to increase your income, lower outgo, and control future spending. This may mean selling assets and making sacrifices. When you have done everything you can, pray for God to give you peace about sharing your need with a family member or relative. When you have that peace, don't ask them for money. Simply ask for their permission to share your circumstances with them, as you would like their advice. What would they do if they were in your position? They may give you several options; they may even offer to help you.

If they don't help you with a loan, thank them and love them just the same. Then continue to pray for God's direction for your next step.

If God does not supply your need through a loan consolidation, He may want you to learn by working it out the hard way—month by month with each creditor. God knows that some people need to learn the hard way. According to a survey, 75 percent of those who obtained a loan consolidation ended up right back where they were in twelve months' time because they did not overcome ignorance with wisdom and did not change their attitude about spending, borrowing, and living within their income.

Summary

Our summary comment on loans is: Do not borrow if you can avoid doing so. **If you do borrow, get out of debt as soon as possible.** Seek godly counsel to learn to put together a budget plan that helps you get out and stay out of debt.

CHAPTER 17
HOW BOB AND SUE
BALANCED THEIR BUDGET

As you have seen in the sample forms throughout this book, before counseling, Bob and Sue's outgo exceeded their income by $610 per month. Plus they took an average of $74 per month from their savings and borrowed $1,200 just to make ends meet. In addition, they were increasing their debt by using credit cards. While they wanted to give 10 percent to God, they were only giving 3 percent. They wanted to increase their savings, but they were spending part of their existing savings.

Obviously, many changes needed to take place in the next year if they were going to accomplish their goals, which were to honor the Lord with 10 percent, get out of debt, stay out of debt, provide for the family, and save for the future. After counseling they overcame their ignorance by learning God's wisdom on managing money. Next came a major decision on their part: "Are we going to apply God's direction in our daily financial plan? If so, we need to change our attitude about money and money matters."

They learned God's way to manage money and made the decision to change their attitude and obey God's way. The following paragraphs indicate the step-by-step decisions they made that resulted in a balanced budget that enhanced their love, joy, peace, and contentment as they worked toward their goals.

Income

After Bob and Sue's decision to change their attitude about borrowing, spending, and living within their income, God began to bless them. Bob received a 10 percent increase in his salary. Sue received an increase of $2,076 per year. They also decided not to borrow any more money and not to plan on any more gifts to meet their budget needs. After reviewing their tax withholding, they lowered the amount withheld on their W-4 forms so they would eliminate their usual tax refund. They realized that the refund could be better used payday by payday to balance their budget. Because they were going to increase their savings on a regular basis with their new plan, the interest they would earn would increase from $5 per month to $10 per month. The net income from all sources would increase from $3,000 to $3,130 per month.

Outgo

1. Bob and Sue immediately started to give 10 percent of their gross income to God—from $90 per month to $313 per month, an increase of $2,676 per year.

2. They did a projected tax return at the beginning of the year and lowered their withholding to plan for an estimated break-even point so there would be no refund and no amount owed for the next filing period. Even with an increase in taxable income of $4,224, they could reduce their withholding from $444 to $437 per month.

3. They refinanced their home at a lower interest rate and lowered the payment from $621 to $421 per month. They also paid all past-due payments and paid off the auto loan in full from the refinance proceeds. They also shopped for a better rate on their homeowner's insurance policy and reduced the premium from $384 to $336 per year. They projected an increase of $24 in their real estate tax. They estimated that they could reduce their electric bill from $107 to $97 per month by lowering their hot water thermostat and installing a timer to heat it only when they needed it hot. They decided to reduce the number and length of long-distance calls to cut the phone bill in

half, from $62 to $36 per month. The water bill and the trash removal rates were set rates, so no change could be made in those two items. They decided to do more of the house maintenance themselves and reduce the expense from $41 to $36 per month. It was a hard decision, but they canceled cable TV and eliminated the $23 per month expense. They also decided to get by with their present furniture and not spend any money next year on furniture, which eliminated $32 per month. The net result of all their changes in the housing category resulted in a reduction from $1,068 to $770 per month, or a savings of $3,576 per year.

4. Bob and Sue started shopping for food by a list prepared at home and then stuck to their list. They also used coupons, but only for the items already on the list. Before using any coupons, they shopped for the best price of other brands, including the store brand products. They also changed their diets by reducing the purchase of snacks and drinks, and they decided washing dishes was cheaper than buying paper cups and plates. The end result was a reduction of $31 per month, or $372 per year, at the grocery store.

5. One of their tougher decisions was whether to sell an auto and eliminate the auto payment of $288 per month or to borrow $6,912 more on their home refinance to pay off the auto loan. They decided to borrow $6,912 more on the home to eliminate the auto payment. This allowed them to take a greater interest deduction on their tax return. They also decided to reduce their unnecessary driving and combine all their shopping to one time per week or on their way to or from work to lower the cost for gasoline from $96 to $84 per month. They also shopped for a better rate on auto insurance and lowered their premium from $288 to $222 for a six-month premium. Bob also decided to do some of the minor auto repairs himself to lower their auto maintenance expense by an estimated $192 per year. The net result of their changes in the auto category reduced their expenses by $327 per month, or $3,924 per year.

6. They made no change on their life or health insurance but decided to trust the Lord and canceled their disability insurance, which saved them $132 per year.

7. They decided to take $2,229 from the home refinance and pay all past-due payments in the All Other Debt category. This paid in full a credit card balance and a debt to a doctor, which were both due in full. In an effort to get out of debt as soon as possible, they decided to prepay by $144 per month on the remaining debts in the All Other Debt category. Their plan was to pay $427 per month instead of the contracted amount of $283 per month.

8. As they analyzed their entertainment and recreation activities, they agreed to dine out less often and cut back slightly on their vacation. When they cut back on their evening out activities, doing so also cut back on the babysitter expense. They also decided to reduce their video rentals by 50 percent. The hard decision was to sell the boat to eliminate all boat expenses. Their net reduction in the entertainment and recreation category was $876 per year.

9. To cut back on their clothing expense, they decided to buy only what they absolutely needed and to shop for bargain sales and shop at discount shops. They were amazed at how little they really "needed" when they took inventory of their closet and dresser drawers. They decided to stop any impulse buying and browsing for clothes. Their projected savings in this category was $120 per year.

10. Bob and Sue knew the trend had to be reversed in the savings category. Last year they took out $888, which averaged $74 per month. The guideline amount to save for their level of income was $116 per month, but they put a higher priority on getting out of debt, so they prepaid their All Other Debt category by $144 per month and cut back their monthly savings from $116 to $54 per month. Another reason was that they already had an existing savings balance of $1,200. Their net change in savings was from taking out $74 per month to adding $54 per month, which was an effective increase of $128 per month, or $1,536 per year.

11. While the guideline amount to invest was $185 per month for their level of income, they decided to defer any investments until they paid off all debts in the All Other Debt category of $8,378 and had an amount in their savings equal to three months' gross income ($3,130 x 3 = $9,390). They estimated two years to pay off the $8,378 and another year to achieve their savings goal.

12. While Bob and Sue's medical expenses were normally low due to their good health, the past year was higher than usual, primarily due to the stress brought on by their financial pressures. Now that the financial pressures were removed with their new budget, they reduced their projected expense for medical from $87 to $35 per month, or a reduction of $624 per year.

13. In the Miscellaneous category, they made changes where they could. They cut back on their drugstore item spending and decided to trim hair at home between haircuts at the shop. They decided to carry their lunch more often to reduce their lunch money spending. They discontinued magazine subscriptions and cut gift buying to nearly one-half of their previous spending. They also cut their pocket money spending by one-half. Their final

cutback was to find another home for their pet. The net reduction of Miscellaneous spending was $116 per month, or $1,392 per year.

As you can see, it took the knowledge of a guide, the wisdom of godly counsel, the changed attitudes of Bob and Sue, and finally their commitment to establish a plan (the budget) and to follow the plan before the problem was solved. It didn't happen overnight! It took one day at a time, one decision after another, and one item at a time to balance the budget.

Bob and Sue found out that biblical principles applied to everyday finances really work! They were banking on the Bible for a balanced budget, and it happened. It was all here, in *Family Money Management God's Way*, and it is here for you.

APPENDIX A
COST-CUTTING HINTS

Housing

Mortgage

- Consider renting part of your home to someone else.
- Consider possible refinancing to lower interest rate and lower payment.

Rent

- Shop for lower rental payments.
- Consider renting part of your home to someone else.

Home Insurance

- Shop and compare for the best possible terms and rates.
- Do not overpay to your mortgage escrow account for home insurance.
- Consider increasing the deductible amount.

Real Estate Taxes

- Compare the real estate tax assessor's appraisal of your home with other comparable home values. If you are overassessed, ask for a reconsideration.
- Do not overpay to your mortgage escrow account for real estate taxes.

Electric/Gas/Oil

- Check attic for insulation; doors and windows for air leaks; change filters regularly.
- Keep thermostat set at moderate comfort levels.
- Delay using heat or cool air until necessary. Use sweaters, blankets, or fans.
- Close off any part of the home not used frequently.
- Turn off unused lights; reduce bulb wattage in nonwork or nonreading areas.
- Group bath times to conserve hot water.
- Insulate all exposed hot water lines and your hot water heater.
- Reduce your hot water heater thermostat(s) from 140 to 120 degrees.
- Reduce the number of hours you heat hot water (manually or with a timer).

- Avoid partial load use of dishwasher, washer, and dryer—use a full load.
- Stop dishwasher before drying cycle—allow dishes to dry by themselves.
- Group your cooking and baking while stove and oven are hot.
- Consider solar energy to heat water.

Telephone

- Evaluate need for more than one home phone and for cell phones.
- Use plain standard phone, no frills, no extra features.
- Limit the number and length of all long-distance calls.
- Make long-distance calls during reduced rate times.
- Write more letters and make fewer long-distance calls.

Water and Sewage

- Conserve use of water when washing dishes and hands and brushing teeth.
- Conserve use of water when bathing (shorter showers).
- Use well water when and where applicable.
- Turn off hose when not needed to wash cars, boat, and house.
- Repair all leaks promptly.

Maintenance

- Do your own house and lawn pest control.
- Reduce use of fertilizer—use natural organic materials.
- Do your own plumbing, electric, carpentry, and other repairs.
- Mow, edge, trim, and maintain your own lawn.
- Rent the equipment and clean your own carpets and furniture.
- Do your own painting and wallpapering.

Cable TV

- Consider using standard local stations only.
- Next consider using the basic cable only.
- Avoid "Pay for View" and unnecessary extra-tier channels.

Furniture

- Shop for best buys—sales, discontinued items.
- Consider repairing, refinishing, and recovering used good-quality furniture.
- Shop the local shopper's guide, garage sales, and thrift stores.
- Consider making your own furniture.

Appliances

- Maintain what you have—consult service manuals.
- Keep written maintenance charts.

- Do not overload or abuse appliances. Follow instructions.
- Learn to be a do-it-yourselfer. Seek counsel when available.
- Before replacing, consider a repair or overhaul. Many older units are better quality and cost less to repair.
- If replacing, use a buyer's guide to determine the best manufacturer.
- Stick to standard models. More dials and gadgets usually cost more and usually require more maintenance.
- Shop and compare price, quality, and service. Keep a written record.
- Look for high-volume dealers who carry name-brand products under their own label at lower prices.
- Buy on a cash basis. Avoid trade-ins. Seek discounts for cash.
- Avoid dealer service contracts—usually expensive and no guarantee that they will be in business when you are in need.
- Seek free delivery and installation.
- Look for similar used units in the paper or shopper's guide.

Food

- Shop by a written list only—prepared at home.
- Buy larger quantities, which usually cost less per ounce.
- Shop less frequently—every week or every two weeks.
- Avoid buying when hungry.
- Leave children and spouse at home.
- Only use coupons for items on your need list.
- Only use coupons after shopping for price—not label.
- Also shop for price per serving. Compare canned, frozen, and fresh.
- Reduce or eliminate paper products.
- Compare the price of drugstore-type items at food stores with discount chain stores. Usually, but not always, they are cheaper at discount stores.
- Avoid sugar-coated higher priced cereals. They are usually more expensive but not more nutritious.
- Avoid prepared foods, TV dinners, potpies, cakes. You are paying more for expensive labor that you can supply.
- Avoid food plans that package and deliver large quantities of meats. You will end up eating more meat, which in the long run will cost you more, especially if you buy their overpriced freezer to go with it.
- Compare store brand prices with the more popular brands.
- Buy items when in season to get the lowest prices.
- Shop for advertised specials but be sure products really are "on sale," not just "as advertised" but the same old price.
- Consider making your own baby food.
- Consider canning your own fresh vegetables.
- Consider buying in bulk with other families.
- Consider serving your family "restaurant style" not family style—only one plate per meal filled in the kitchen—no extra food on the table.

- Consider buying items advertised as buy one, get one free—if it is on your list or an item you frequently use that has a long shelf life.

Auto

- Learn to perform your own routine maintenance—oil change, lubrication, etc.
- Perform preventative maintenance over the more costly corrective maintenance.
- Purchase your parts and supplies from wholesale distributors for the best grades and prices.
- Maintain a written regular maintenance chart or list for every car to extend the life of your cars (up to 40 percent).
- Consider buying "take-off" tires from dealers who frequently change tires on new cars or on fleets of cars.
- Use the cheapest gasoline rated for your car.
- Buy only what you can pay for in cash—avoid financing.
- Consider repairing your old car, as the cost of repairs are almost always cheaper than buying and financing a new car.
- If it is really time to buy another car, consider a newer but less expensive car. Many cars can be bought for half the price when three to four years old.
- Before buying any car, new or newer than your present car, check your budget to see how much cash you have and how much you can afford to pay monthly.
- Avoid buying another car if your present car is not paid in full. That leads to upside-down financing and additional costs of refinancing, especially if the payoff is computed on the rule of 78s.
- Realize that it is usually better to bargain for a discount on the purchase of your new car and pay cash for it than to buy on the "trade-in" plan.
- If you do finance your new car purchase, shop for the best financing available, not just the quickest and easiest offered by the dealer.
- If you buy a used car, talk to the previous owner before you buy. Also have it checked by your mechanic before you buy.
- Bargain for a short-term 100 percent guarantee if you buy a used car.
- Avoid being pressured by sales tactics. Set your own price and car type desired and stick to your plan, even if it means walking away from a so-called good deal that requires a quick decision.
- Be willing to accept minor problems or repairs on older cars.
- Avoid buying a new model when they first come out. It is better to wait for a demonstrator or year-end closeout sale.
- Note that the standard model usually provides the same transportation as the luxury model and at a substantial savings.
- Avoid the use of credit life insurance. It is expensive and unnecessary if you have an adequate overall insurance program.
- Note that extended warranties are also expensive and should not be necessary if you are buying a quality car.
- The average family should avoid new car leasing, as it is always more expensive in the long run. If you can't afford a down payment, you most likely can't afford the car at this time.

Insurance

Life

- Seek godly counsel to establish an overall insurance plan for your present income and your specific needs and goals. GET THE FACTS!
- Establish a budget to determine how much insurance you need. GET THE FACTS!
- Select a plan that meets your needs and fits your budget. GET THE FACTS!
- Get godly counsel from several qualified people, but recognize that you are responsible for your decision. Decide after getting the facts and praying for God's direction, which usually comes in the form of a lasting peace about your decision.
- Buy insurance to provide for your family if you are unable to provide from your estate, which is your abundance.

Health

- Again, seek godly counsel.
- Determine your need.
- Get the facts!
- Select a plan that fits your income and need.
- Buy what you can afford and need.
- Consider a major medical plan that insures the big-ticket liability, not every pill and every doctor visit, unless you can afford the low-deductible all-expenses-paid policy offered by your insurance company.

Debts

- Establish a plan to get out and stay out of debt.
- Stop using credit cards, except for convenience, and pay the balance IN FULL every month.
- Decide to pay cash from this day on.
- Save for the future at the same time you are paying off your debts.
- Be fair to every creditor. Pay each one every dollar.
- Do not leave any creditor out of your current plan.
- If you are past due with any creditor, contact them, apologize for breaking your promise to pay the minimum required amount, and advise them of your plan to repay all past-due payments—and make all future required payments on time as agreed. Then keep your promise and follow your plan.
- Make as many sacrifices as necessary to follow your plan until you are current with all creditors.
- Seek options to increase your income, lower your outgo, and control your future spending until you reach your goals.

Entertainment and Recreation

Dining Out

- Dine out less frequently and at less expensive places.
- Order only water to drink and avoid the expensive beverages when eating out.
- Use discount, early-bird, or two-for-one specials when they fit your time and budget plan.
- Establish your budget and the specific amount you have allocated for dining out. Then select a plan of places to go and limits to pay.

Trips/Vacation

- Plan vacations during off-season, if possible, when rates are lower.
- Consider camping to avoid higher motel and restaurant costs.
- Select vacations close to home; they give you more time to recreate and cost less for travel.
- Consider swapping your house with a relative or a Christian family in another town for your vacation.
- Stay at home and change the daily routine and activities for the entire family.
- If flying, plan in advance and buy supersaver tickets or special fare plans.
- Consider a working vacation where the whole family spends part of every day painting the house or doing some other project together.

Babysitting

- Find one or more couples with children and trade off babysitting for each other at no cost.
- Barter for sitters. You fix their hair or mow their lawn; they sit for your children.

Activities

- Plan activities like hiking, camping, swimming at the lake or beach, etc., that have minimum expense.
- Attend movies, bowling, or other activities during hours of lower admission fees.
- Get two or more families together to share video rentals.
- Carpool to nearby towns for special sporting events.
- Volunteer to help serve food at children's school sports events and get free admission.
- Swap your boat for your friend's camper for a week.

Clothing

- Make some clothing for you and the children as time and talent permit.
- Buy from a need list only, prepared at home after looking in the closets.
- Buy during the "off" season when prices are their lowest.
- Buy basic outfits that you can mix and match, dress up or dress down.
- Shop at discount outlets and for special sales.

- Buy hand- and machine-washable fabrics to avoid dry cleaning costs.
- Repair any damaged clothing early.
- Take good care of your existing clothing.
- Pass hand-me-downs among friends and family.
- Shop garage sales and thrift stores for real bargains.

Savings

- Use an automatic withdrawal (payroll deduction) when possible.
- Pay your savings account just as you would a creditor.
- Save for a purpose. Set your goals. Start saving NOW.
- Set a fixed amount to be saved, regularly, based on your budget.
- Possible savings goals: to build an estate; to buy a home, car, furniture, appliance; to take a vacation; to make a home or auto repair; to be able to help others with a gift or loan.
- Save one specific amount for the future—not to be spent.
- Save another specific amount as a reserve to be spent for the variety of other purposes you are saving.

Investments

- The purpose of every investment should be to bring glory to God.
- Investments are longer-term savings usually for a specific purpose, such as pensions, college education, etc.
- Use automatic withdrawal (payroll deduction) when possible.
- Set a fixed amount to be invested based on your budget.
- One type investment provides you with an income now.
- Another type investment simply grows and only provides you with the increase when sold.
- Some investment earnings are taxable now.
- Other investment earnings are tax deferred.
- Some investments are made through financial institutions. Other investments are made direct to individuals.
- Where applicable, both husband and wife should agree on the investments before they are made.
- Every investment has a degree of risk.
- Every investor should seek a balance between convenience, availability, rate of return, and safety.
- Do not invest in anything you don't understand.
- Consider investing in your own family.
- One of your best investments is to get out of debt.

Medical Expenses

- Take good care of yourself and your family. Preventative action is less expensive than corrective action.
- Select physicians and dentists who practice preventative care.
- Get estimates of costs in advance. When practical, get second opinions.
- Shop for price on prescriptions, glasses, etc.
- Read books and articles on proper health care and nutrition.

Miscellaneous

Drugstore Items

- Shop for price on each item and from various type sources; compare grocery stores, drugstores, discount stores, direct sales, etc.
- Always shop from a needs list prepared at home after looking in all your closets.
- Compare price per ounce or per unit and buy the larger quantity or size when it proves to be the best buy.

Beauty Parlor/Barber Shop

- Do your hair care at home when possible; trim your spouse's hair in between haircuts, and learn to cut your children's hair.
- Stretch the time between hair appointments.

Laundry/Dry Cleaners

- Buy clothing that doesn't need to be dry cleaned.
- Use coin-operated dry clean machines when available.
- Use full loads, not partial and not overloaded, in coin-operated laundry machines.
- Buy your own washer and dryer as soon as possible, even used, as it is cheaper to do laundry yourself at home.
- Dry your own clothes on a line in lieu of a dryer.

Lunch

- Pack your lunch for children and yourself.
- Drink water only for lunch.
- Avoid buying special lunch-size packaged foods that are usually very expensive. Make and package your own.
- Use reusable containers for packing lunches. Avoid more expensive throwaways.

Allowances

- Avoid allowances. Only reward children for extra work performed, not the usual expected chores, such as picking up their clothes, cleaning their rooms, helping with dishes, etc., which is part of their responsibility as a member of the family.

- Give your children an opportunity to work and earn money. Select special projects, such as washing windows, washing and waxing the car, mowing the lawn, and babysitting, etc., to earn money in lieu of a set allowance for doing nothing.

Subscriptions

- Reduce or eliminate periodical subscriptions (paper, magazines, books, records, etc.).
- If a subscription is continued, use longer-term contracts (two to three years), which are usually less expensive.
- Swap subscriptions with neighbors, friends, or family.

Gifts

- Limit your gifts in number and amount per gift.
- Buy on a cash basis. Avoid using credit or credit cards.
- Make personal gifts (plaques, paintings, and poems, etc.).
- Make a written calendar list of known birthdays, anniversaries, and holidays; set a dollar amount for each based on your budget allocation for gifts; stick to your budget amount.
- Consider cards or letters in lieu of gifts.
- Consider baked goods as gifts when appropriate.
- In large families, draw names for exchanging gifts.
- Remember to honor the Lord at Christmas. It is His birthday. Find creative ways to honor the Lord.
- Have your children select a gift they would like, and then have them earn money to buy it and give it to a needy child their gender and age.
- Shop by list only for Christmas, predetermine the amount to spend on each gift, and stick to your list and amount.
- Remember, buy on a cash basis, not credit.
- Mail packages early and use the least expensive carrier to deliver.

Education

- Determine the amount available based on your budget.
- Gather the facts about all the options.
- Decide on the school based on the best academically that your budget can afford.
- Save in advance. Avoid borrowing for education.
- Have your student participate in the expense by working part-time job(s), especially for college education.
- Evaluate need for value of and interest in special lessons, music, dance, etc.
- Seek scholarships and grants that may be available.
- Carpool to reduce transportation costs when applicable.
- Buy used books in lieu of new books when available.
- Have your student avoid owning a car while in college, if possible.
- Teach your college student to establish and live on a budget.

- Do not allow your student to use credit cards.

Pocket Money

- Set a regular specific amount, weekly, based on the budget.
- Stick to that amount.
- Avoid impulse spending for drinks, snacks, gum, etc.
- Decide in advance what to buy with your pocket money.
- Avoid being wasteful or buying unnecessary items.
- Milk, bread, gas, etc., are not considered miscellaneous pocket money items. These already have specific budget categories.

Pet Store/Veterinarian

- Consider the cost of keeping a pet before buying.
- Limit your purchases to the pet's needs and your budget.
- Shop for best veterinarian fees.
- Have children participate in providing for their pet care.

Other

- Shop for the best bank services. Avoid service charges.
- Learn to prepare your own income taxes.
- Shop for fees if you need to use an attorney.
- Shop for child-care rates. Consider bartering.
- Keep the required minimum balance in your checking account to avoid service charges and returned check fees.
- Carry no credit cards, checks, or extra cash unless you have a planned purchase that day.

APPENDIX B
BUDGET FORMS

NOTE: FOR MAXIMUM BENEFIT read the entire book, read the instructions, and refer to the samples before completing the forms!

Step Number	Instructions and Sample for	Form Description	Page
1	Form No. 1	Past Income and Outgo	30
2	Form No. 2	Current Income and Outgo	35
3	Form No. 3	List of Debts	39
4	Form No. 1	Projected Income	43
5	Form No. 4	Monthly Budget Guide	44
6	Chart 5.1	Percentage Guide	45
7	Form No. 5	Budget Analysis	49
8	Form No. 1	Projected Outgo	52
9	Form No. 5	Projected Monthly Budget	54
10	Form No. 6	Options to Increase Income	57
11	Form No. 7	Options to Lower Outgo	59
12	Form No. 8	Options to Control Spending	61
13	Form No. 2	Budget Control	66
14	Form No. 1	Paycheck Breakdown	70
15	Chart 10.1	Paycheck Breakdown	71
16	Chart 10.2	Paycheck Breakdown for Husband and Wife	72

NOTE:

Forms may be reproduced for personal use before using the last blank form. Following this page are two blank perforated pages of each form, numbers 1 through 8, except for Form 2, which has twelve blank copies for a twelve-month supply. Remember, use pencil on ALL blank forms.

AVERAGE MONTHLY INCOME AND OUTGO FOR THE PAST CALENDAR YEAR

PAST   PROJECTED   FROM _____ TO _____

GROSS INCOME PER MONTH _____ [ ]

- Salary, Pension, Soc Sec (His) _____ [ ]
- Salary, Pension, Soc Sec (Hers) _____ [ ]
- Interest and dividends _____ [ ]
- Net from Investments/Rents _____ [ ]
- Gifts and Inheritance _____ [ ]
- Tax Refunds _____ [ ]
- Other _____ [ ]

OUTGO PER MONTH

1. Tithe and Offering _____ [ ]
2. Taxes (IRS - Soc. Sec.-Med.) _____ [ ]

NET SPENDABLE INCOME _____ [ ]
(GROSS INCOME MINUS LINES 1 & 2)
ALSO LIST ON LINE A BELOW)

3. Housing _____ [ ]
- Mortgage (Rent) _____ [ ]
- House Insurance _____ [ ]
- Real Estate Taxes _____ [ ]
- Electricity / Gas / Oil _____ [ ]
- Telephone _____ [ ]
- Water & Sewage _____ [ ]
- Trash Removal _____ [ ]
- Maintenance _____ [ ]
- Cable TV _____ [ ]
- Other _____ [ ]

4. Food (Grocery Store) _____ [ ]
5. Auto (Transportation) _____ [ ]
- Payments _____ [ ]
- Gas _____ [ ]
- Auto Insurance _____ [ ]
- License Tag _____ [ ]
- Repairs / Maintenance _____ [ ]
- Vehicle Replacement _____ [ ]

6. Insurance _____ [ ]
- Life _____ [ ]
- Health _____ [ ]
- Other _____ [ ]

7. DEBTS _____ [ ] ✳
- Credit Cards _____ [ ]
- Installment Loans _____ [ ]
- Other _____ [ ]

8. Enter/Recreation _____ [ ]
- Dining Out _____ [ ]
- Trips / Vacation _____ [ ]
- Babysitters _____ [ ]
- Activities _____ [ ]
- Video Rentals _____ [ ]
- Other _____ [ ]

9. Clothing (Cash) _____ [ ]
10. Savings (+or-) _____ [ ] ✳
11. Investments (+or-) _____ [ ] ✳
12. Medical Expenses _____ [ ]
- Doctor _____ [ ]
- Dentist _____ [ ]
- Prescriptions _____ [ ]
- Other _____ [ ]

13. Miscellaneous _____ [ ]
- Drugstore Items _____ [ ]
- Beauty / Barber _____ [ ]
- Laundry / Dry Cleaning _____ [ ]
- Lunch (Work / School) _____ [ ]
- Subscriptions _____ [ ]
- Gifts (Incl Christmas) _____ [ ]
- Special Education _____ [ ]
- Pocket Money _____ [ ]
- Pet Store / Veterinarian _____ [ ]
- Other _____ [ ]

TOTAL EXPENSES (3-13) _____ [ ]
(ALSO LIST ON LINE B BELOW)

A. NET SPENDABLE INCOME _____ [ ]
B. LESS EXPENSES (3-13) _____ [ ]
C. DIFFERENCE/MONTH (+OR-) _____ [ ]
(LINE A MINUS LINE B)
D. DIFFERENCE/YEAR (+OR-) _____ [ ]
(MULTIPLY LINE C X 12)

INSTRUCTIONS

Insert only "Past" income and outgo on the lines—after chapter 7 insert only "Projected" income and outgo in the boxes.

Use pencil—use the most accurate figures possible. Fill every blank; if no amount, insert a dash (—).

Round all figures off to the nearest dollar (for example, 941.36 should be 941, and 941.82 should be 942).

Convert all weekly figures to monthly (for example, $100/week x 52 weeks = $5,200/year ÷ 12 months = $433/month).

If self-employed do NOT include business income and use only your net profit from the business that was brought home for the family's use.

✳ Do these 3 projections last and divide your abundance among them only when planning your budget projections.

FORM #1

AVERAGE MONTHLY INCOME AND OUTGO FOR THE PAST CALENDAR YEAR

PAST   PROJECTED   FROM _____ TO _____

GROSS INCOME PER MONTH _____ [ ]

- Salary, Pension, Soc Sec (His) ____ [ ]
- Salary, Pension, Soc Sec (Hers) ____ [ ]
- Interest and dividends ____ [ ]
- Net from Investments/Rents ____ [ ]
- Gifts and Inheritance ____ [ ]
- Tax Refunds ____ [ ]
- Other _____ [ ]

OUTGO PER MONTH

1. Tithe and Offering _____ [ ]

2. Taxes (IRS - Soc. Sec.-Med.) ____ [ ]

NET SPENDABLE INCOME _____ [ ]
(GROSS INCOME MINUS LINES 1 & 2)
ALSO LIST ON LINE A BELOW)

3. Housing _____ [ ]

- Mortgage (Rent) ____ [ ]
- House Insurance ____ [ ]
- Real Estate Taxes ____ [ ]
- Electricity / Gas / Oil ____ [ ]
- Telephone ____ [ ]
- Water & Sewage ____ [ ]
- Trash Removal ____ [ ]
- Maintenance ____ [ ]
- Cable TV ____ [ ]
- Other _____ [ ]

4. Food (Grocery Store) ____ [ ]

5. Auto (Transportation) ____ [ ]

- Payments ____ [ ]
- Gas ____ [ ]
- Auto Insurance ____ [ ]
- License Tag ____ [ ]
- Repairs / Maintenance ____ [ ]
- Vehicle Replacement ____ [ ]

6. Insurance ____ [ ]

- Life ____ [ ]
- Health ____ [ ]
- Other _____ [ ]

7. DEBTS _____ [ ] ✳

- Credit Cards ____ [ ]
- Installment Loans ____ [ ]
- Other _____ [ ]

8. Enter/Recreation _____ [ ]

- Dining Out ____ [ ]
- Trips / Vacation ____ [ ]
- Babysitters ____ [ ]
- Activities ____ [ ]
- Video Rentals ____ [ ]
- Other _____ [ ]

9. Clothing (Cash) ____ [ ]

10. Savings (+or-) ____ [ ] ✳

11. Investments (+or-) ____ [ ] ✳

12. Medical Expenses ____ [ ]

- Doctor ____ [ ]
- Dentist ____ [ ]
- Prescriptions ____ [ ]
- Other _____ [ ]

13. Miscellaneous ____ [ ]

- Drugstore Items ____ [ ]
- Beauty / Barber ____ [ ]
- Laundry / Dry Cleaning ____ [ ]
- Lunch (Work / School) ____ [ ]
- Subscriptions ____ [ ]
- Gifts (Incl Christmas) ____ [ ]
- Special Education ____ [ ]
- Pocket Money ____ [ ]
- Pet Store / Veterinarian ____ [ ]
- Other _____ [ ]

TOTAL EXPENSES (3-13) ____ [ ]
(ALSO LIST ON LINE B BELOW)

A. NET SPENDABLE INCOME ____ [ ]

B. LESS EXPENSES (3-13) ____ [ ]

C. DIFFERENCE/MONTH (+OR-) ____ [ ]
(LINE A MINUS LINE B)

D. DIFFERENCE/YEAR (+OR-) ____ [ ]
(MULTIPLY LINE C X 12)

INSTRUCTIONS

Insert only "Past" income and outgo on the lines—after chapter 7 insert only "Projected" income and outgo in the boxes.

Use pencil—use the most accurate figures possible. Fill every blank; if no amount, insert a dash (—).

Round all figures off to the nearest dollar (for example, 941.36 should be 941, and 941.82 should be 942).

Convert all weekly figures to monthly (for example, $100/week x 52 weeks = $5,200/year ÷ 12 months = $433/month).

If self-employed do NOT include business income and use only your net profit from the business that was brought home for the family's use.

✳ Do these 3 projections last and divide your abundance among them only when planning your budget projections.

FORM #1

CURRENT MONTHLY INCOME AND OUTGO RECORD

USE PENCIL — Record every penny daily.

Beginning Cash $ _____
Beginning Checking $ _____

Ending Cash $ _____
Ending Checking $ _____

← PROJECTED BUDGET →

		1 TITHE (GOD)	2 TAXES (GOV'T.)	3 HOUSING	4 FOOD GROCERY	5 AUTO	6 INSURANCE	7 DEBTS	8 ENTER. REC.	9 CLOTHING	10 SAVINGS	11 INVESTMENTS	12 MEDICAL	13 MISC.	PROJECTED OUTGO
GROSS INCOME ALL SOURCES	MONTH / YEAR	DESCRIPTION OF COLUMNS #1—#12													DESCRIPTION OF MISC. ONLY #13
	1														
	2														
	3														
	4														
	5														
	6														
	7														
	8														
	9														
	10														
	11														
	12														
	13														
	14														
	15														
	16														
	17														
	18														
	19														
	20														
	21														
	22														
	23														
	24														
	25														
	26														
	27														
	28														
	29														
	30														
	31														
TOTAL INCOME ↓	← MONTHLY TOTALS →														TOTAL OUTGO #1—#13
↓	ADD BEGINNING CASH, CHECKS AND TOTAL MONTHLY INCOME	←PROOF TOTALS→													ADD ENDING CASH, CHECKING, TOTAL OUTGO→
	PROJECTED BUDGET LESS MONTHLY TOTALS														

FORM #2

CURRENT MONTHLY INCOME AND OUTGO RECORD
USE PENCIL — Record every penny daily.

Beginning Cash $ _____
Beginning Checking $ _____

Ending Cash $ _____
Ending Checking $ _____

GROSS INCOME ALL SOURCES	← PROJECTED BUDGET →		1 TITHE (GOD)	2 TAXES (GOV'T)	3 HOUSING	4 FOOD GROCERY	5 AUTO	6 INSURANCE	7 DEBTS	8 ENTER. REC.	9 CLOTHING	10 SAVINGS	11 INVESTMENTS	12 MEDICAL	13 MISC.	PROJECTED OUTGO	DESCRIPTION OF MISC. ONLY #13
	DESCRIPTION OF COLUMNS #1—#12	MONTH															
		YEAR															
		1															
		2															
		3															
		4															
		5															
		6															
		7															
		8															
		9															
		10															
		11															
		12															
		13															
		14															
		15															
		16															
		17															
		18															
		19															
		20															
		21															
		22															
		23															
		24															
		25															
		26															
		27															
		28															
		29															
		30															
		31															
↓	MONTHLY TOTALS →	TOTAL INCOME															TOTAL OUTGO #1—#13
↓	ADD BEGINNING CASH, CHECKS AND TOTAL MONTHLY INCOME														←PROOF TOTALS→		ADD ENDING CASH, CHECKING, TOTAL OUTGO→
	PROJECTED BUDGET LESS MONTHLY TOTALS																	

FORM #2

CURRENT MONTHLY INCOME AND OUTGO RECORD

USE PENCIL — Record every penny daily.

Beginning Cash $ _____
Beginning Checking $ _____

Ending Cash $ _____
Ending Checking $ _____

GROSS INCOME ALL SOURCES	MONTH / YEAR	PROJECTED BUDGET → DESCRIPTION OF COLUMNS #1—#12	1 TITHE (GOD)	2 TAXES (GOV'T)	3 HOUSING	4 FOOD GROCERY	5 AUTO	6 INSURANCE	7 DEBTS	8 ENTER. REC.	9 CLOTHING	10 SAVINGS	11 INVESTMENTS	12 MEDICAL	13 MISC.	PROJECTED OUTGO DESCRIPTION OF MISC. ONLY #13
	1															
	2															
	3															
	4															
	5															
	6															
	7															
	8															
	9															
	10															
	11															
	12															
	13															
	14															
	15															
	16															
	17															
	18															
	19															
	20															
	21															
	22															
	23															
	24															
	25															
	26															
	27															
	28															
	29															
	30															
	31															
TOTAL INCOME ↓		MONTHLY TOTALS →														TOTAL OUTGO #1—#13
↓ ADD BEGINNING CASH, CHECKS AND TOTAL MONTHLY INCOME														←PROOF TOTALS→		←PROOF TOTALS ADD ENDING CASH, CHECKING, TOTAL OUTGO→
PROJECTED BUDGET LESS MONTHLY TOTALS																

FORM #2

CURRENT MONTHLY INCOME AND OUTGO RECORD

USE PENCIL — Record every penny daily.

Beginning Cash $ _____
Beginning Checking $ _____

Ending Cash $ _____
Ending Checking $ _____

← PROJECTED BUDGET →

MONTH		GROSS INCOME ALL SOURCES	DESCRIPTION OF COLUMNS #1—#12	1 TITHE (GOD)	2 TAXES (GOV'T.)	3 HOUSING	4 FOOD GROCERY	5 AUTO	6 INSURANCE	7 DEBTS	8 ENTER. REC.	9 CLOTHING	10 SAVINGS	11 INVESTMENTS	12 MEDICAL	13 MISC.	PROJECTED OUTGO	DESCRIPTION OF MISC. ONLY #13
YEAR																		
1																		
2																		
3																		
4																		
5																		
6																		
7																		
8																		
9																		
10																		
11																		
12																		
13																		
14																		
15																		
16																		
17																		
18																		
19																		
20																		
21																		
22																		
23																		
24																		
25																		
26																		
27																		
28																		
29																		
30																		
31																		
TOTAL INCOME ←		← MONTHLY TOTALS →																TOTAL OUTGO #1—#13
←	ADD BEGINNING CASH, CHECKS AND TOTAL MONTHLY INCOME													←PROOF TOTALS→				ADD ENDING CASH, CHECKING, TOTAL OUTGO→
	PROJECTED BUDGET LESS MONTHLY TOTALS																	

FORM #2

CURRENT MONTHLY INCOME AND OUTGO RECORD

USE PENCIL — Record every penny daily.

Beginning Cash $ _____
Beginning Checking $ _____

Ending Cash $ _____
Ending Checking $ _____

← PROJECTED BUDGET →

PROJECTED OUTGO

GROSS INCOME ALL SOURCES	MONTH / YEAR	DESCRIPTION OF COLUMNS #1—#12	1 TITHE (GOD)	2 TAXES (GOV'T)	3 HOUSING	4 FOOD GROCERY	5 AUTO	6 INSURANCE	7 DEBTS	8 ENTER. REC.	9 CLOTHING	10 SAVINGS	11 INVESTMENTS	12 MEDICAL	13 MISC.	DESCRIPTION OF MISC. ONLY #13
	1															
	2															
	3															
	4															
	5															
	6															
	7															
	8															
	9															
	10															
	11															
	12															
	13															
	14															
	15															
	16															
	17															
	18															
	19															
	20															
	21															
	22															
	23															
	24															
	25															
	26															
	27															
	28															
	29															
	30															
	31															
TOTAL INCOME ←		← MONTHLY TOTALS →														TOTAL OUTGO #1—#13

← ADD BEGINNING CASH, CHECKS AND TOTAL MONTHLY INCOME

← PROOF TOTALS →

ADD ENDING CASH, CHECKING, TOTAL OUTGO →

PROJECTED BUDGET LESS MONTHLY TOTALS

FORM #2

CURRENT MONTHLY INCOME AND OUTGO RECORD

USE PENCIL — Record every penny daily.

Beginning Cash $ _____
Beginning Checking $ _____

Ending Cash $ _____
Ending Checking $ _____

← PROJECTED BUDGET →

GROSS INCOME ALL SOURCES

MONTH														PROJECTED OUTGO
YEAR	DESCRIPTION OF COLUMNS #1—#12	1 TITHE (GOD)	2 TAXES (GOV'T)	3 HOUSING	4 FOOD GROCERY	5 AUTO	6 INSURANCE	7 DEBTS	8 ENTER. REC.	9 CLOTHING	10 SAVINGS	11 INVESTMENTS	12 MEDICAL	13 MISC.	DESCRIPTION OF MISC. ONLY #13

Rows numbered 1 through 31.

TOTAL INCOME → MONTHLY TOTALS → TOTAL OUTGO #1—#13 →

ADD BEGINNING CASH, CHECKS AND TOTAL MONTHLY INCOME ←PROOF TOTALS→ PROOF TOTALS → ADD ENDING CASH, CHECKING, TOTAL OUTGO→

PROJECTED BUDGET LESS MONTHLY TOTALS

FORM #2

CURRENT MONTHLY INCOME AND OUTGO RECORD

USE PENCIL — Record every penny daily.

Beginning Cash $ _____
Beginning Checking $ _____

Ending Cash $ _____
Ending Checking $ _____

		PROJECTED BUDGET →	1 TITHE (GOD)	2 TAXES (GOV'T)	3 HOUSING	4 FOOD GROCERY	5 AUTO	6 INSURANCE	7 DEBTS	8 ENTER. REC.	9 CLOTHING	10 SAVINGS	11 INVESTMENTS	12 MEDICAL	13 MISC.	PROJECTED OUTGO	DESCRIPTION OF MISC. ONLY #13
MONTH	YEAR	DESCRIPTION OF COLUMNS #1—#12															
1																
2																
3																
4																
5																
6																
7																
8																
9																
10																
11																
12																
13																
14																
15																
16																
17																
18																
19																
20																
21																
22																
23																
24																
25																
26																
27																
28																
29																
30																
31																

GROSS INCOME ALL SOURCES ←

TOTAL INCOME ← | MONTHLY TOTALS → | | TOTAL OUTGO #1—#13

ADD BEGINNING CASH, CHECKS AND TOTAL MONTHLY INCOME ← | PROOF TOTALS → | ← PROOF TOTALS → | ADD ENDING CASH, CHECKING, TOTAL OUTGO →

PROJECTED BUDGET LESS MONTHLY TOTALS

FORM #2

CURRENT MONTHLY INCOME AND OUTGO RECORD

USE PENCIL — Record every penny daily.

Beginning Cash $ _____

Beginning Checking $ _____

Ending Cash $ _____

Ending Checking $ _____

PROJECTED BUDGET →

PROJECTED OUTGO

DESCRIPTION OF COLUMNS #1—#12

DESCRIPTION OF MISC. ONLY #13

	1 TITHE (GOD)	2 TAXES (GOV'T.)	3 HOUSING	4 FOOD GROCERY	5 AUTO	6 INSURANCE	7 DEBTS	8 ENTER. REC.	9 CLOTHING	10 SAVINGS	11 INVESTMENTS	12 MEDICAL	13 MISC.

MONTH _____

YEAR _____

GROSS INCOME ALL SOURCES

Rows 1–31

← TOTAL INCOME → ← MONTHLY TOTALS →

← ADD BEGINNING CASH, CHECKS AND TOTAL MONTHLY INCOME

← PROOF TOTALS →

TOTAL OUTGO #1—#13

ADD ENDING CASH, CHECKING, TOTAL OUTGO →

PROJECTED BUDGET LESS MONTHLY TOTALS

FORM #2

CURRENT MONTHLY INCOME AND OUTGO RECORD
USE PENCIL — Record every penny daily.

Beginning Cash $ _____

Beginning Checking $ _____

Ending Cash $ _____

Ending Checking $ _____

GROSS INCOME ALL SOURCES	PROJECTED BUDGET → DESCRIPTION OF COLUMNS #1—#12	1 TITHE (GOD)	2 TAXES (GOV'T.)	3 HOUSING	4 FOOD GROCERY	5 AUTO	6 INSURANCE	7 DEBTS	8 ENTER. REC.	9 CLOTHING	10 SAVINGS	11 INVESTMENTS	12 MEDICAL	13 MISC.	PROJECTED OUTGO DESCRIPTION OF MISC. ONLY #13
MONTH															
YEAR															
1															
2															
3															
4															
5															
6															
7															
8															
9															
10															
11															
12															
13															
14															
15															
16															
17															
18															
19															
20															
21															
22															
23															
24															
25															
26															
27															
28															
29															
30															
31															
TOTAL INCOME ↓	MONTHLY TOTALS →														TOTAL OUTGO #1—#13
↓	ADD BEGINNING CASH, CHECKS AND TOTAL MONTHLY INCOME										←PROOF TOTALS →				←PROOF TOTALS
	PROJECTED BUDGET LESS MONTHLY TOTALS														ADD ENDING CASH, CHECKING, TOTAL OUTGO→

FORM #2

CURRENT MONTHLY INCOME AND OUTGO RECORD

USE PENCIL — Record every penny daily.

Beginning Cash $ _____
Beginning Checking $ _____

Ending Cash $ _____
Ending Checking $ _____

← PROJECTED BUDGET →

PROJECTED OUTGO

MONTH YEAR	1 TITHE (GOD)	2 TAXES (GOV'T)	3 HOUSING	4 FOOD GROCERY	5 AUTO	6 INSURANCE	7 DEBTS	8 ENTER. REC.	9 CLOTHING	10 SAVINGS	11 INVESTMENTS	12 MEDICAL	13 MISC.	DESCRIPTION OF MISC. ONLY #13
GROSS INCOME ALL SOURCES / DESCRIPTION OF COLUMNS #1—#12														
1														
2														
3														
4														
5														
6														
7														
8														
9														
10														
11														
12														
13														
14														
15														
16														
17														
18														
19														
20														
21														
22														
23														
24														
25														
26														
27														
28														
29														
30														
31														
TOTAL INCOME ← / MONTHLY TOTALS →														TOTAL OUTGO #1—#13
↓ ADD BEGINNING CASH, CHECKS AND TOTAL MONTHLY INCOME	←PROOF TOTALS→												ADD ENDING CASH, CHECKING, TOTAL OUTGO→	
PROJECTED BUDGET LESS MONTHLY TOTALS														

FORM #2

CURRENT MONTHLY INCOME AND OUTGO RECORD
USE PENCIL — Record every penny daily.

Beginning Cash $ _____
Beginning Checking $ _____

Ending Cash $ _____
Ending Checking $ _____

PROJECTED BUDGET →

DESCRIPTION OF COLUMNS #1—#12	MONTH / YEAR	1 TITHE (GOD)	2 TAXES (GOV'T)	3 HOUSING	4 FOOD GROCERY	5 AUTO	6 INSURANCE	7 DEBTS	8 ENTER. REC.	9 CLOTHING	10 SAVINGS	11 INVESTMENTS	12 MEDICAL	13 MISC.	PROJECTED OUTGO	DESCRIPTION OF MISC. ONLY #13
GROSS INCOME ALL SOURCES																
	1															
	2															
	3															
	4															
	5															
	6															
	7															
	8															
	9															
	10															
	11															
	12															
	13															
	14															
	15															
	16															
	17															
	18															
	19															
	20															
	21															
	22															
	23															
	24															
	25															
	26															
	27															
	28															
	29															
	30															
	31															
TOTAL INCOME ←	← MONTHLY TOTALS →														TOTAL OUTGO #1—#13	
↓	ADD BEGINNING CASH, CHECKS AND TOTAL MONTHLY INCOME										←PROOF TOTALS →				ADD ENDING CASH, CHECKING, TOTAL OUTGO→	
	PROJECTED BUDGET LESS MONTHLY TOTALS															

FORM #2

CURRENT MONTHLY INCOME AND OUTGO RECORD

USE PENCIL — Record every penny daily.

Beginning Cash $ _____
Beginning Checking $ _____

Ending Cash $ _____
Ending Checking $ _____

← PROJECTED BUDGET →

GROSS INCOME ALL SOURCES	MONTH	YEAR	1 TITHE (GOD)	2 TAXES (GOV'T.)	3 HOUSING	4 FOOD GROCERY	5 AUTO	6 INSURANCE	7 DEBTS	8 ENTER. REC.	9 CLOTHING	10 SAVINGS	11 INVESTMENTS	12 MEDICAL	13 MISC.	PROJECTED OUTGO
DESCRIPTION OF COLUMNS #1—#12																DESCRIPTION OF MISC. ONLY #13
1																
2																
3																
4																
5																
6																
7																
8																
9																
10																
11																
12																
13																
14																
15																
16																
17																
18																
19																
20																
21																
22																
23																
24																
25																
26																
27																
28																
29																
30																
31																
TOTAL INCOME ↓	← MONTHLY TOTALS →															TOTAL OUTGO #1—#13

↑ ADD BEGINNING CASH, CHECKS AND TOTAL MONTHLY INCOME ← PROOF TOTALS → ADD ENDING CASH, CHECKING, TOTAL OUTGO →

PROJECTED BUDGET LESS MONTHLY TOTALS

FORM #2

LIST OF DEBTS

as of _____
date prepared

	1 TO WHOM OWED	2 USED FOR WHAT	3 CURRENT UNPAID BALANCE	4 DOLLAR AMOUNT PAST DUE	5 CONTRACT MONTHLY PAYMENT	6 INTEREST RATE (APR)
HOUSING (Primary home only)						
1						
2						
3						

HOUSING TOTAL ⟶

	1 TO WHOM OWED	2 USED FOR WHAT	3 CURRENT UNPAID BALANCE	4 DOLLAR AMOUNT PAST DUE	5 CONTRACT MONTHLY PAYMENT	6 INTEREST RATE (APR)
AUTO (Do Not Include Business Vehicles)						
1						
2						
3						

AUTO TOTAL ⟶

ALL OTHER DEBTS (List from the largest balance down to the smallest balance)

1						
2						
3						
4						
5						
6						
7						
8						
9						
10						
11						
12						
13						
14						
15						
16						
17						
18						
19						
20						
21						
22						
23						
24						

ALL OTHER DEBTS TOTAL ⟶

(Do **NOT** include housing and auto total in this total)

INSTRUCTIONS: Use pencil—Round all figures to the nearest dollar.
If self-employed do NOT include business debts.
You should have 3 separate totals for the 3 different categories of debt.

FORM #3

LIST OF DEBTS

as of _____
date prepared

	1 TO WHOM OWED	2 USED FOR WHAT	3 CURRENT UNPAID BALANCE	4 DOLLAR AMOUNT PAST DUE	5 CONTRACT MONTHLY PAYMENT	6 INTEREST RATE (APR)
HOUSING (Primary home only)						
1						
2						
3						

HOUSING TOTAL ⟶

AUTO (Do Not Include Business Vehicles)						
1						
2						
3						

AUTO TOTAL ⟶

ALL OTHER DEBTS (List from the largest balance down to the smallest balance)

1						
2						
3						
4						
5						
6						
7						
8						
9						
10						
11						
12						
13						
14						
15						
16						
17						
18						
19						
20						
21						
22						
23						
24						

ALL OTHER DEBTS TOTAL ⟶
(Do **NOT** include housing and auto total in this total)

INSTRUCTIONS: Use pencil—Round all figures to the nearest dollar.
If self-employed do NOT include business debts.
You should have 3 separate totals for the 3 different categories of debt.

FORM #3

MONTHLY BUDGET GUIDE

Date Completed _____

A. **PROJECTED** GROSS AVERAGE **MONTHLY** INCOME (from form #1) $ _____

B. **PROJECTED** GROSS **ANNUAL** INCOME (Line A x 12) $ _____

BUDGET CATEGORIES 1.	FROM 2. PERCENTAGE GUIDE	from Line A 3. GROSS MONTHLY INCOME	YOUR 4. GUIDE (nearest dollar)
1. Tithe (God)	____% X	$_____ =	$_____
2. Taxes (Gov't)	____% X	$_____ =	$_____

C.   TOTAL OF CATEGORIES 1. & 2. = $ _____

D. NET SPENDABLE INCOME (Line A minus Line C) $ _____

BUDGET CATEGORIES	FROM PERCENTAGE GUIDE	from Line D NET MONTHLY INCOME	YOUR GUIDE (nearest dollar)
3. Housing	____% X	$_____ =	$_____
4. Food	____% X	$_____ =	$_____
5. Auto	____% X	$_____ =	$_____
6. Insurance	____% X	$_____ =	$_____
7. Debts	____% X	$_____ =	$_____
8. Enter/Recreation	____% X	$_____ =	$_____
9. Clothing	____% X	$_____ =	$_____
10. Savings	____% X	$_____ =	$_____
11. Investment	____% X	$_____ =	$_____
12. Medical	____% X	$_____ =	$_____
13. Miscellaneous	____% X	$_____ =	$_____

E. **NET SPENDABLE TOTAL** (Total of Categories 3-13, should equal line D.) $ _____

INSTRUCTIONS:
Use pencil. Use nearest dollar amount. Use **gross monthly income** in column 3 for categories 1 & 2. Use **net spendable income** in column 3 for categories 3-13. Gross incomes below $30,000 do **NOT** have a percentage in the investment category. Use the best estimate for your projected gross average monthly income on Line A. This is NOT YOUR budget, or your limit, only a guide for your income level. DO NOT change any percent from the guide.

FORM #4

MONTHLY BUDGET GUIDE

Date Completed _____

A. <u>PROJECTED</u> GROSS AVERAGE <u>MONTHLY</u> INCOME (from form #1) $ _____

B. <u>PROJECTED</u> GROSS <u>ANNUAL</u> INCOME (Line A x 12) $ _____

BUDGET CATEGORIES 1.	FROM 2. PERCENTAGE GUIDE	from Line A 3. GROSS MONTHLY INCOME	YOUR 4. GUIDE (nearest dollar)
1. Tithe (God)	_____ % X	$ _____ =	$ _____
2. Taxes (Gov't)	_____ % X	$ _____ =	$ _____

C.   TOTAL OF CATEGORIES 1. & 2. = $ _____

D. NET SPENDABLE INCOME (Line A minus Line C) $ _____

BUDGET CATEGORIES	FROM PERCENTAGE GUIDE	from Line D NET MONTHLY INCOME	YOUR GUIDE (nearest dollar)
3. Housing	_____ % X	$ _____ =	$ _____
4. Food	_____ % X	$ _____ =	$ _____
5. Auto	_____ % X	$ _____ =	$ _____
6. Insurance	_____ % X	$ _____ =	$ _____
7. Debts	_____ % X	$ _____ =	$ _____
8. Enter/Recreation	_____ % X	$ _____ =	$ _____
9. Clothing	_____ % X	$ _____ =	$ _____
10. Savings	_____ % X	$ _____ =	$ _____
11. Investment	_____ % X	$ _____ =	$ _____
12. Medical	_____ % X	$ _____ =	$ _____
13. Miscellaneous	_____ % X	$ _____ =	$ _____

E. **NET SPENDABLE TOTAL** (Total of Categories 3-13, should equal line D.) $ _____

INSTRUCTIONS:

Use pencil. Use nearest dollar amount. Use **gross monthly income** in column 3 for categories 1 & 2. Use **net spendable income** in column 3 for categories 3-13. Gross incomes below $30,000 do **NOT** have a percentage in the investment category. Use the best estimate for your projected gross average monthly income on Line A. This is NOT YOUR budget, or your limit, only a guide for your income level. DO NOT change any percent from the guide.

FORM #4

BUDGET ANALYSIS

Date Completed _____

COLUMN	1 PAST MONTHLY BUDGET (FROM FORM #1)	2 MONTHLY BUDGET GUIDE (FROM FORM #4)	3 DIFFERENCE (SUBTRACT COLUMN 2 FROM COLUMN 1) + IF OVER GUIDE − IF UNDER GUIDE	4 order of difference	5 PROJECTED MONTHLY BUDGET
A. GROSS MONTHLY INCOME	$	$	▓▓▓▓▓▓		$
1. TITHE (God) (OFFERINGS)					
2. TAXES (Gov't) (IRS - SS - MED)					
B. NET SPENDABLE INCOME (GROSS MINUS CATEGORIES 1 & 2)	$	$	▓▓▓▓▓▓		$
3. HOUSING					
4. FOOD					
5. AUTO					
6. INSURANCE					
7. DEBTS					
8. ENTER/RECREATION					
9. CLOTHING					
10. SAVINGS					
11. INVESTMENTS					
12. MEDICAL					
13. MISCELLANEOUS					
C. TOTALS (3-13 only)	$	$	▓▓▓▓▓▓		$
DIFFERENCE (B minus C)	$				

INSTRUCTIONS:

Use pencil. Use nearest dollar amount. Complete column #1 from form #1, column #2 from form #4, and place the difference in column #3. To complete column #4 disregard the (+) and (−) in column #3 and number the differences from the largest difference #1 to the smallest difference #13, **DO NOT** complete column #5 until you have read chapter 7 and completed your new projected budget in the boxes on form #1. When your new projected budget is completed on form #1 then transfer your figures from form #1 to column #5, Form #5 above.

FORM #5

BUDGET ANALYSIS

Date Completed _____

COLUMN	1	2	3	4	5
	PAST MONTHLY BUDGET (FROM FORM #1)	MONTHLY BUDGET GUIDE (FROM FORM #4)	DIFFERENCE (SUBTRACT COLUMN 2 FROM COLUMN 1) + IF OVER GUIDE – IF UNDER GUIDE	order of difference	PROJECTED MONTHLY BUDGET
A. GROSS MONTHLY INCOME	$	$	░░░░░░░░		$
1. TITHE (God) (OFFERINGS)					
2. TAXES (Gov't) (IRS - SS - MED)					
B. NET SPENDABLE INCOME (GROSS MINUS CATEGORIES 1 & 2)	$	$	░░░░░░░░		$
3. HOUSING					
4. FOOD					
5. AUTO					
6. INSURANCE					
7. DEBTS					
8. ENTER/RECREATION					
9. CLOTHING					
10. SAVINGS					
11. INVESTMENTS					
12. MEDICAL					
13. MISCELLANEOUS					
C. TOTALS (3-13 only)	$	$	░░░░░░░░		$
DIFFERENCE (B minus C)	$				

INSTRUCTIONS:

Use pencil. Use nearest dollar amount. Complete column #1 from form #1, column #2 from form #4, and place the difference in column #3. To complete column #4 disregard the (+) and (–) in column #3 and number the differences from the largest difference #1 to the smallest difference #13, **DO NOT** complete column #5 until you have read chapter 7 and completed your new projected budget in the boxes on form #1. When your new projected budget is completed on form #1 then transfer your figures from form #1 to column #5, Form #5 above.

FORM #5

OPTIONS TO INCREASE YOUR PRESENT INCOME

DATE #1	#2 #	POSSIBLE OPTIONS #3	DATE #4	ACTIONS TAKEN AND RESULTS #5
	1			
	2			
	3			
	4			
	5			
	6			
	7			
	8			
	9			
	10			
	11			
	12			
	13			
	14			
	15			
	16			
	17			
	18			
	19			
	20			

INSTRUCTIONS: List the date and the possible option on the left side. (List any option that God brings to mind.) Now pray over this list until God gives you a peace about taking action on one or more options then list the date, the action taken, and the results on the right side on the line with the option. Keep adding options day by day as God brings more options to mind, and keep praying over this list daily.

SOME POSSIBLE OPTIONS: Second job, odd jobs, overtime on present job, higher paying position with present employer, different higher paying primary job, spouse take employment, older children take part-time employment, sell assets not needed, hold garage sales, gifts from family, turn hobby into income producer.
PLEASE BE CREATIVE IN PREPARING YOUR LIST.

FORM #6

OPTIONS TO INCREASE YOUR PRESENT INCOME

DATE [#1]	# [#2]	POSSIBLE OPTIONS [#3]	DATE [#4]	ACTIONS TAKEN AND RESULTS [#5]
	1			
	2			
	3			
	4			
	5			
	6			
	7			
	8			
	9			
	10			
	11			
	12			
	13			
	14			
	15			
	16			
	17			
	18			
	19			
	20			

INSTRUCTIONS: List the date and the possible option on the left side. (List any option that God brings to mind.) Now pray over this list until God gives you a peace about taking action on one or more options then list the date, the action taken, and the results on the right side on the line with the option. Keep adding options day by day as God brings more options to mind, and keep praying over this list daily.

SOME POSSIBLE OPTIONS: Second job, odd jobs, overtime on present job, higher paying position with present employer, different higher paying primary job, spouse take employment, older children take part-time employment, sell assets not needed, hold garage sales, gifts from family, turn hobby into income producer.
PLEASE BE CREATIVE IN PREPARING YOUR LIST.

FORM #6

OPTIONS TO LOWER YOUR EXISTING OUTGO

DATE #1	# #2	POSSIBLE OPTIONS #3	DATE #4	ACTIONS TAKEN AND RESULTS #5
	1			
	2			
	3			
	4			
	5			
	6			
	7			
	8			
	9			
	10			
	11			
	12			
	13			
	14			
	15			
	16			
	17			
	18			
	19			
	20			

INSTRUCTIONS: List the date and the possible option on the left side. (List any option that God brings to mind.) Now pray over this list until God gives you a peace about taking action on one or more options then list the date, the action taken, and the results on the right side on the line with the option. Keep adding options day by day as God brings more options to mind, and keep praying over this list daily.

SOME POSSIBLE OPTIONS: Reduce your spending and apply the surplus to your debts; increase your income and apply the surplus to your debts; ask each creditor to lower your monthly payment; sell any asset not needed and on which you are still making payments, then pay off the debt from the proceeds of that sale; loan consolidation or refinancing.
PLEASE BE CREATIVE IN PREPARING YOUR LIST.

FORM #7

OPTIONS TO LOWER YOUR EXISTING OUTGO

DATE #1	#2 #	POSSIBLE OPTIONS #3	DATE #4	ACTIONS TAKEN AND RESULTS #5
	1			
	2			
	3			
	4			
	5			
	6			
	7			
	8			
	9			
	10			
	11			
	12			
	13			
	14			
	15			
	16			
	17			
	18			
	19			
	20			

INSTRUCTIONS: List the date and the possible option on the left side. (List any option that God brings to mind.) Now pray over this list until God gives you a peace about taking action on one or more options then list the date, the action taken, and the results on the right side on the line with the option. Keep adding options day by day as God brings more options to mind, and keep praying over this list daily.

SOME POSSIBLE OPTIONS: Reduce your spending and apply the surplus to your debts; increase your income and apply the surplus to your debts; ask each creditor to lower your monthly payment; sell any asset not needed and on which you are still making payments, then pay off the debt from the proceeds of that sale; loan consolidation or refinancing.
PLEASE BE CREATIVE IN PREPARING YOUR LIST.

FORM #7

ز

OPTIONS TO CONTROL YOUR FUTURE SPENDING

DATE #1	# #2	POSSIBLE OPTIONS #3	DATE #4	ACTIONS TAKEN AND RESULTS #5
	1			
	2			
	3			
	4			
	5			
	6			
	7			
	8			
	9			
	10			
	11			
	12			
	13			
	14			
	15			
	16			
	17			
	18			
	19			
	20			

INSTRUCTIONS: List the date and the possible option on the left side. (List any option that God brings to mind.) Now pray over this list until God gives you a peace about taking action on one or more options then list the date, the action taken, and the results on the right side on the line with the option. Keep adding options day by day as God brings more options to mind, and keep praying over this list daily.

SOME POSSIBLE OPTIONS: Shop from a need list only until budget allows for wants and desires; use coupons for items on need list only; prepare need list at home after looking in the pantry, closet and garage; compare prices of other brands before using coupons; cut back in **all** budget categories; shop less frequently and combine your shopping trips; control impulse spending by carrying **NO** credit cards, **NO** checks, and **NO** extra cash, carry **only** the cash needed for that days' planned spending.

PLEASE BE CREATIVE IN PREPARING YOUR LIST.

FORM #8

OPTIONS TO CONTROL YOUR FUTURE SPENDING

DATE #1	#2 #	POSSIBLE OPTIONS #3	DATE #4	ACTIONS TAKEN AND RESULTS #5
	1			
	2			
	3			
	4			
	5			
	6			
	7			
	8			
	9			
	10			
	11			
	12			
	13			
	14			
	15			
	16			
	17			
	18			
	19			
	20			

INSTRUCTIONS: List the date and the possible option on the left side. (List any option that God brings to mind.) Now pray over this list until God gives you a peace about taking action on one or more options then list the date, the action taken, and the results on the right side on the line with the option. Keep adding options day by day as God brings more options to mind, and keep praying over this list daily.

SOME POSSIBLE OPTIONS: Shop from a need list only until budget allows for wants and desires; use coupons for items on need list only; prepare need list at home after looking in the pantry, closet and garage; compare prices of other brands before using coupons; cut back in **all** budget categories; shop less frequently and combine your shopping trips; control impulse spending by carrying **NO** credit cards, **NO** checks, and **NO** extra cash, carry **only** the cash needed for that days' planned spending.

PLEASE BE CREATIVE IN PREPARING YOUR LIST.

FORM #8

ABOUT THE AUTHOR

Mahlon Hetrick was born in Hershey, Pennsylvania, and lived in Washington, D.C., for twenty-five years. He and his wife, Marlyn, moved to Fort Myers, Florida, in 1959. They have three sons, Gary, Daniel, and Kenneth. Mahlon served in the U.S. Army in Korea, and he is a Dale Carnegie graduate and a graduate of the Savings and Loan School for Executive Development at the University of Georgia. His teaching career includes management, communication, and personal finance courses at Edison Community College and biblical financial counseling at Gulf Shore Christian College and Brethren Biblical Institute.

For many years, Mahlon Hetrick served as a community leader; he is a past president of several organizations. He also served in the church as a deacon, teacher, and finance committee chairman, and beyond the church as a past chairman of the Christian Businessmen's Committee in Fort Myers.

He has been honored by the Fort Myers Board of Realtors, the Lee County Chamber of Commerce, and Edison Community College for outstanding service. The National Secretaries Association named him Boss of the Year in 1974–75. After spending most of his thirty years in banking as a senior officer, he founded Christian Financial Counseling, a nonprofit corporation, and serves as its director, senior counselor, and president of the board.

Mahlon counsels with hundreds of counselees per year on a nonfee basis; plus he gives seminars and workshops and serves as a speaker for many groups and organizations, primarily throughout the state of Florida. For several years he has appeared on radio and television talk shows. Hundreds of satisfied counselees refer their friends and family members to Christian Financial Counseling because they have seen God's Word work as it has been compassionately taught by the author. Pastors who have experienced the financial seminars presented by Mahlon have enthusiastically recommended the seminars to other churches.

MAY WE HEAR FROM YOU?

If you would like to receive our bimonthly newsletter, at least one donation per year of any amount will put you on and keep you on our bimonthly mailing list. Our newsletter contains current articles on money-related subjects, a personal testimony, daily scripture reading, and our calendar of events.

If you have any questions, comments, suggestions, or criticisms about this workbook, we welcome your honest evaluation, which should help us to improve our next printing. Is there any subject that you would like to see included in future books or pamphlets?

If this book has been helpful for you, one of the highlights of our newsletter is the testimony of a counselee who has listened to God's counsel and followed His direction in obedience, which then resulted in God's blessing. We can include your testimony in future publications in part or in full and of course in confidence, using fictitious names, if you write and share your financial blessings from God.

We thank you kindly for your interest in this book and shall appreciate every response from you for any reason. May God bless you richly for your obedience to His Word and His ways to manage money.

In His Love,
Mahlon

Direct all correspondence to:

Christian Financial Counseling, Inc.
2267 First St. Unit 15
Fort Myers, FL 33901-2954

Phone: (239) 337-2122
Fax: (239) 337-2134
E-mail: Cfcministry7@cs.com
Web site: www.cfcswf.org